Incorporating Erotic Kink into Your Lifestyle

Educational and training guide for beginners and enthusiasts.

Includes a glossary of BDSM terms, a list of commonly used acronyms, safety tips, a training questionnaire, and a basic M/s or D/s contract.

By Leonard Cascia

"What dreams we dare to dream within ourselves that we fear may come true."

Table of Contents

Introduction

BDSM activity is becoming more and more mainstream. A recent sociologist report published in the Journal of Sexual Medicine regards this as a leisure activity; for some it is, and for others it's simply a way of life. The report states that those who engage in BDSM activity develop a sense of personal freedom, enjoyment, improved personal skills, a sense of adventure, self-expression, positive emotions, and decreased stress levels.

I have seen over the past few years that more and more new people are introducing themselves into this form of erotic activity at various levels, and they all ask the same question: Where do I begin?

This book will help answer many of those questions you have. Some of you may just want to tip your toe in the waters, so to speak, while others will just jump right in.

There are tens of thousands of variations on the dynamics of this lifestyle, and it would be impossible to list them all. I have written this guide as a way for you, the reader, to get a foothold on many of the basics and dynamic possibilities involved in BDSM. Some of you may only be interested in bondage and domination, while others wish to incorporate the full spectrum that BDSM has to offer. I have included a glossary of terms, a questionnaire, and a standard M/s – D/s contract template. There is also a list of commonly used acronyms.

This is a guidebook on your journey into the erotic world of BDSM, and will help you overcome fear and the many misconceptions. I have also included some safety tips to help further you along your journey.

Play smart, play safe, and journey well,

~ LC

Don't just play — play well, play smart and most of all, play safe.

Consent is a requirement from both ends of the leash.

About the Author

I have played and studied BDSM for many years, starting in my mid-20s. I'm currently in my late 50s as of this publication, and I'm still going strong. I kept my activities for the majority of those years behind closed doors, out of the clubs and off the web. I have only recently "come out of the closet," so to speak.

Chapter 1:

Dispelling Myths & Misconceptions

Before I begin, let's go through just what BDSM means. BDSM is short for Bondage, Discipline & Sadomasochism. Practiced by consenting adults in a wide variety of ways, this book will help give you a better general understanding of this common practice.

What does Bondage and Discipline have to do with physical sex? Nothing. What does Sadomasochism have to do with physical sex? Nothing.

Erotica for the mind, stretching your fantasies beyond your own comprehension at times. It's only when you — as a consenting, individual adult — decide to incorporate physical sex into your BDSM activity that this element comes into play.

For the sake of any future arguments, I will refer to Masters, Dominants, and Mistresses as "Dom's" in general, and submissives and slaves will be referred to as "s-types." These serve as larger umbrella terms under which the more specific terms fit.

A special note for everyone reading this book: No one can read your minds, no one has any magical crystal ball. I have come across enough people who seem to be under the impression that every Dom or s-type should already know this or that piece of information or personal preference. It is important never to make assumptions about anyone's knowledge based solely on whatever label or title they have given themselves.

I personally view the s-types as empowering themselves through their submission. It takes a lot of courage, trust, and respect to kneel before someone, or to allow them to collar, dominate, or otherwise control you, and it is wise for an s-type to always remember this fact.

Likewise, a Dom should never take their s-types offerings or attempts for granted. The symbiotic relationship statuses that form between a Dom and s-type are equal, yet different. One could not be without the other.

Outsiders commonly referred to in the kink community as "vanilla," or non-BDSM oriented people, can sometimes view this activity as abusive, controlling, and manipulative — even psychologically damaging to one's mental health.

The truth could not be further from this negative image. These are loving, caring and nurturing people who simply wish to indulge themselves in their erotic, kinky desires in healthy and consensual ways. They are answering that call from within themselves to explore their erotic or fetishistic desires. They seek to fulfill and satisfy that curiosity about themselves — and not always in a sexual way.

These are everyday people you see strolling down the street, shopping, or at your place of work. People from all walks of life, all backgrounds. Our minds are our biggest sex organ and should be satisfied as well as our bodies. Getting our head into subspace, that altered state of mind after a particularly intense scene, is an experience well worth pursuing.

From my own personal experiences, subspace was like physically being in a beautiful, blissful place; a wonderful lucid dream. It is typically brought on in BDSM activities by the release of endorphins in the human body through pain.

I was getting a tattoo, however, when it first happened to me. Ask a thousand different people in the community about subspace and you will get a thousand different answers. It's a very personal experience, one that can touch your very soul.

Some have described it as having an out-of-body experience, with their minds completely disconnected from their bodies, free to travel anywhere in the infinite universe. Those of you who practice deep meditation may have experienced such an event yourselves: an out-of-body experience like no other.

Getting there is the journey of exploring yourself and your willingness to challenge and overcome your fears. BDSM is a journey of exploring the mind and body.

The road lies ahead of you. Journey well.

Basics and Rules

Doesn't it seem that the more civilized we have all become, the more we drift away from our primal needs and desires? To satisfy our minds, not just our physical desires is necessary; the self-righteous morality of today's society thumbs its judgmental nose at those who dare to engage in this lifestyle. Religions throughout history have themselves engaged in some form of BDSM, and yet in today's modern world, many would deny it ever happened.

Take, for instance, the book *Erotica Universalis*. Within this book, you'll find kinks and fetishes that have roots throughout recorded history, dating back to over 5,000 years ago. From cave men drawings to distinguished noble gentleman, many were getting their kink on before the term we know — BDSM — was ever invented.

I'm sure you've heard the words "sick," "twisted," "perverted," and of course, the old two favorites, "crazy" and "psycho." Despite the stigma and rose-colored illusions, there are, in fact, good perverts and bad perverts. Let me expand on this briefly for you.

There are four simple rules you should play by, and best practice all comes down to consent.

Rule 1 — Never do anything with anyone without their consent.

Rule 2 — Never do anything with anyone without giving them informed consent. Consent is not enough; you both must be on the same page and knowledgeable as to what you both agreed to do. This process is commonly referred to as negotiating. This applies to any type of relationship, and not just with a play partner.

Rule 3 — Never do anything with anyone who is underage. Here in the US, that typically means under the age of 18. Those who are not considered adults cannot legally consent to any sexual activity, whether it contains BDSM or not.

Rule 4 — Never do anything with anyone who is either mentally or physically incapable of giving you consent, whether temporarily or permanently incapacitated or otherwise unable to make such a decision for themselves.

These rules are as much common sense to vanilla people (those outside the BDSM community) as to those of us in the kink community. You need to embrace these rules. Live and play by them. It all comes down to self-discipline, self-control, and common sense.

Another question those of us in the community hear a lot: "But isn't BDSM just an excuse for abuse?"

Not at all. Vanilla or BDSM relationships can feature abusive tendencies and behavior as much as any other, but this is a sign of a bad relationship or a toxic partner, not a healthy practice of good, safe, and consensual BDSM. That BDSM is inherently abusive could not be further from the truth.

The following list helps explains the difference between healthy BDSM and abuse.

BDSM vs. Abuse

BDSM with consent: The use of various implements or techniques with informed consent to elicit a physical sensation and/or to heighten mental awareness.

Abuse: To inflict physical pain and mental anguish on a person that harms them physically and/or emotionally without their consent.

BDSM with consent: A mutual understanding of a consensual exchange of power where all parties involved have openly negotiated. Generally described as "informed consent."

Abuse: Takes away the power and rights from the victim thru force without their consent.

BDSM with consent: Creates excitement and a heighten sense of awareness and pleasure in all parties involved.

Abuse: The abused victim doesn't know where, how or even why at times. No communication. No consent given.

BDSM with consent: Builds trust and respect for all involved. Supportive and respected by all.

Abuse: Violates trust through cruel and inhumane treatment of another human being without their consent.

BDSM with consent: Helps to create open and honest communication between all involved.

Abuse: No communication, no support. The subjugation of another person without their consent and against their will.

BDSM with consent: Has protocols, safety rules, limits, and safe words in place that have been mutually consented and adhered to.

Abuse: Shows no respect to their victim or concern for their safety and well-being. Has no safety protocols, no rules, no safe words.

BDSM with consent: Practiced by responsible, well-informed people who have given their consent.

Abuse: Performed by cowards, egomaniacs, and self-absorbed narcissistic, conceited people. Exhibits immaturity, self-entitlement, and/or bullying behavior.

Performed by responsible consenting adults, BDSM is an outlet that is gratifying to our minds and bodies, **NOT** abuse.

Many of today's vanilla people in a healthy relationship practice some of these rules in one form or another. Those of us who play consensually and responsibly in this lifestyle incorporate two fundamental rule systems: R.A.C.K. and S.S.C. These are the two foundational frameworks on which all BDSM activity is based on, and so these are some key words and phrases to burn into your memory. A glossary of other helpful BDSM terms is listed in Chapter 5 of this book.

R.A.C.K. stands for Risk Aware Consensual Kink; simply put, all parties involved have been made aware of the risks involved and have given their consent.

S.S.C. stands for Safe, Sane, and Consensual. There are tens of thousands of various dynamics as to what someone considerers safe or sane. Everyone is different and, on many different levels, this needs to be thought-out and outlined on an individual basis. This is your personal journey of exploring yourself, and only you can decide on what you like to do or are willing to try. When trying something new, start at the lowest level and work your way up to your limits so that safety is observed and everyone has fun.

Communication is EXTREMELY IMPORTANT! Nether Dom nor s-type should be afraid to speak up or be made to feel inadequate during communication with one another. Communication is the key to a healthy relationship, no matter what kind it is. All people involved should be willing to make whatever adjustments are necessary for what you both personally consider safe and sane play. Dom's have their hard limits just like s-types.

Fetlife.com is a very good group of like-minded people who share their experiences that you can learn from, as well. Just like any group of people anywhere, however, they have their share of assholes, so show any reasonable caution you normally would.

Most Essential Terms and Phrases

<u>Total Power Exchange</u> is for those who live, eat and breathe this lifestyle on a much deeper level. This could include, but is not limited to, physical, emotional, sexual or service-oriented play on levels agreed upon between all parties involved. Some live it 24/7, with or without consensual non-consent agreements. The power exchange should be explored on a level you're both comfortable with. It takes a lot of trust to go full-TPE in a relationship. No one should give someone that level of control over themselves until they have been together for quite a while.

<u>Consensual non-consent</u> is, simply put, the complete surrender of oneself to their Dominant. Dominant commands; s-type obeys. There's a lot of trust involved in this type of relationship. May also be referred to as an Absolute or Total Power Exchange.

<u>Vanilla</u> is the description for anyone or anything not in the BDSM lifestyle, occasionally but not always used in a derogatory manor.

Newbie is someone new and just starting out in the BDSM lifestyle.

Dungeon is a designated room in the home for BDSM scenes or a public or private BDSM club.

A Dungeon Monitor or D.M. is a person who monitors scenes in publics dungeons. Unless someone calls out a safe word and the Dominant player continues without stopping, D.M.s will not typically intervene or interrupt a scene. He or she is there to ensure everyone's safety. A good BDSM club or event sponsor at a club will have a number of D.M.s on hand.

In service refers to someone who is either owned and/or collared by someone, and they may also be in service to someone else but not collared. Play partners are normally not collared, but may be in service to someone. May not be limited to any single person. Example: I loaned out my service slave to another Dom to help clean his kitchen and cook for him while he recovers from surgery.

Collared is a submissive who is owned, property of someone. It is often regarded just as highly as a wedding ring is in the vanilla community. Teenagers and Goth players also wear these, but often only wear it as a decorative piece. Collaring or being collared may or may not involve a collaring ceremony. It is not wise to attempt to play with someone who is collared without first getting permission from the Dominant. Some more private groups use a color code system for collars to prevent miscommunication.

<u>Limits</u> are whatever has been negotiated between all people involved.

<u>Safe words</u> are words or phrases that have been agreed to that either stop or slow down whatever activity is being done. Though some safe words are private and individual, there are also universally known and agreed upon safe words that match traffic lights. When someone calls out the word RED, for instance, all activity stops; YELLOW or MERCY can slow things down when things are getting a bit too intense, but the s-type doesn't wish for the activity to end altogether. Respecting safe words are regarded as sacred in the community and should never be violated. *Saying stop or slow down works just as well for beginners.*

<u>Checking in</u> is any process through which a Dominant may also ask if you're still "green," or okay. This is called checking in, whenever someone seems too far off adrift into sub-space or is having difficulty.

<u>A masochist</u> is someone who enjoys the pleasure that endorphins brings on them through pain.

<u>Endorphins</u> are the body's natural pain killers, released by the human mind throughout the body.

<u>Subspace</u> is an altered sate of being. It can be brought on by many factors and not just through the infliction of pain. Sex, love, service, and emotional fulfillment can bring on subspace, that blissful feeling we all so long for at times in our lives.

Proper etiquette all comes down to the type of relationship of all those involved in an activity. Dominants' protocols and house rules can vary widely and often do. "How do I like my coffee? Handed to me, of course." It's a wise Dominant who keeps a book of protocols and house rules written out so there's no confusion. The excuse "I didn't know" would not be acceptable. *On a special note, a dominant should never punish a submissive for failing a protocol or house rule that was never discussed or spelled out, or who may be sick or injured in some way.*

Munches are groups of like-minded people who gather once or twice a month at a specific place in a vanilla setting. Casual attire is most always requested and playing out BDSM scenes is not allowed. An informal place to meet like-minded new people and discuss everyday events, kink-related issues, and meet new friends or partners.

Contracts are non-legally binding documents, they are unenforceable in any court, but which can help set down all the ground rules and dynamics of a BDSM relationship in a clear way. It's part of the play. Keep in mind, however, that many Dominants and submissives regard a contract as sacred. Some couples regard contracts just as highly as vanilla people regard a marriage license. Some like to incorporate a ceremony of some type prior to its signing. They can be as long or as short as all parties involved wish them to be, and contract titles can be whatever you like them to be: Master / slave, Mistress / slave, Daddy / little, and so on. Don't limit yourself and be as creative as you like with it — it's your contract, after all, and no one can tell you what to include.

s-type is any submissive type of person, but who may not identify themselves as a slave. s-types are also not necessarily masochists. Gender neutral term.

Dominant refers to anyone who identities as a Dom, Master, or Mistress, and is not a gender specific term. Non-males can also identity themselves as Master, some refer to themselves as Mommy Doms, etc. The combination can be whatever you choose to identify yourself as.

Switch refers to someone who switches roles from being a Dominant to a submissive. It can also refer to the act of two partners switching roles during a scene.

Play refers to any BDSM activity that occurs during a scene.

***

These are just a few to get you started, but the glossary contains much, much more.

It's important to remember to research any new activity prior to performing it. Seek out those who have the knowledge and experience. Go to munches and public dungeons, meet people face to face, attend educational training events, watch high-quality YouTube videos, browse Kink.com University's educational videos or at KinkAcademy.com, and so on. Fetlife.com is the largest online community of like-minded people you'll ever find, with thousands of groups listed from all around the world. The Eulenspiegel Society (TES) is an educational nonprofit group, and I highly recommend joining them. They offer many training seminars, and members get a discounted rate.

Reserve your judgment of others' kinks and be respectful of their desires. Many of their kinks might not be for you, some of your own kinks may not be for them. It's considered being vanilla or rude to project your negative judgmental comments onto others, a practice commonly known as "kink-shaming" within the BDSM community. You can always just say, "That kind of kink just isn't for me, but please, enjoy yourself." Different people enjoy different things, and it's important to be respectful.

Why do some people gravitate towards some form of BDSM activity? Everyone has their own reasons as to why. Some are healthy, and some not so healthy. I am not a psychologist by any means. Like in any community, there are good and bad elements. Unfortunately, whenever something bad happens, it hits the news media and everyone gets thrown under the bus together.

You need to be careful when choosing a play partner or meeting for the first time in a public setting. In the early days, let a friend or current partner know the who, what, where, and when of what's happening and set up a specific time to check in. This is referred to as having a **safe call**. Your safe call is your lifeline, so don't ever forgo this step. Should anyone you're meeting or seeing tell you that a safe call isn't needed, I would consider that a very, very big red flag and would avoid ever meeting this person. Dom's, this advice is just as much for you as it is for s-types. s-types are asked to place tremendous faith in you, so treat that growing bond with respect.

***

So, now you've read someone's profile online and decided to make first contact.

Sending private messages is fine, but in writing, nuance is lost, inflection is absent, and misinterpretations can occur when texting each other. There's no reason to not meet face-to-face in a public setting after a couple of weeks if you follow proper safety protocols. There's also no need to waste your time or someone else's if you're not a good fit for one another, so just be honest with yourself and them. Going Dutch is polite with any first meal, and always have a safe call in place just in case.

You're going to come across some red flags and yellow ones, so don't be afraid to ask for clarification on whatever pops up. For the s-type reading this, pay attention. Dom's will typically not be so willing to be your personal service Dom, so be cautious about someone who is too eager to get you alone.

When you do finally get up the courage to contact someone, do keep in mind that they're interviewing you just as much as you're interviewing them.

Responsibility

So just whose responsibility is it anyway? The short answer? Everyone's.

The Dom, the s-type and anyone else with whom you engage, including yourself, in case you were under the impression that you're not, are responsible for everyone's safety. The s-type is only giving up control and is still responsible for engaging and communicating with their Dom. The Dom is just as responsible for communicating with their s-type. It takes two to tango, and you're always responsible for your own actions and safety.

These are the things I expect my Dom or s-type to already know without being told: **Nothing**. unless you have communicated with a specific Dom or s-type, he or she knows absolutely nothing about you or your kinks or knowledge base. We are not mind readers and neither are you. Magical, mind-reading crystal balls aren't real.

"But you pushed me past my limits, why didn't you stop or slow down at least?"

"Because you never called out any safe word, you never asked to stop or slow down, either."

A very reasonable response from an experienced Dom. A newbie s-type might complain endlessly and blame the Dom, or worse, they could simply leave and never communicate anything with you again. So with that in mind and during first play with a newbie, I'm recommending not being so rigid until you both get to know each other better.

I would recommend checking in more often. Simply asking "Are you okay?" regularly can help avoid a small issue from escalating into something bigger. This safety protocol doesn't guarantee that they will call you back, either, of course. People are free to change their minds at any time and it is important to respect a person's ongoing consent.

I'm sure to get a lot of hell from the community for this phrasing, but extreme caution is one of my own personal protocols when it comes to first play with a newbie. Better to be safe than sorry later on if the police show up at your front door. They don't know what bruises are consensual.

Aftercare

Aftercare is an important aspect of all BDSM activity. Your Dom or s-type may be experiencing feelings of shame or guilt after doing a scene. It's important that you comfort your each other and reassure them and yourself that everything is okay, mentally and physically. Check in with them a few days later to make sure they haven't "bottom or Top dropped" (See glossary).

A special note for all Dominants: Once the power exchange has started and you begin your scene, you are completely and 100% responsible after that point. Your s-type has agreed to surrender themselves to your will. You are now in charge.

And for the s-types: Once you have agreed to surrender yourself to another's will, you are 100% responsible for calling out your safe words if you feel the need to.

Avoiding Toxic People

What you should be looking out for in the abusive behaviors of others.

Diversion tactics and manipulation that narcissists, sociopaths, and psychopaths use to silence you.

Some aspects or outward appearances of abusive behavior, on various levels, fall into the realm of BDSM. Degradation, objectification, and humiliation play all feature these qualities in one form or another.

The difference is whether or not you have consented to it with full knowledge and understanding of it. INFORMED CONSENT IS ALWAYS THE KEY PHRASE HERE, FOLKS.

We all, at one time or another, express some form of this behavior as a defense mechanism. That's just normal behavior within certain contexts and no one is a perfect saint, but the ones who constantly behave in these ways outside of consensual agreements are the ones we all need to avoid.

You're both looking for someone you can trust with your body and mind, someone who respects you and your needs and is willing and able to nurture them / appreciate and respect you as a person and an individual. I know this sounds like a no-brainer, but for some people in the thick of real circumstances and conflicting emotions, it's not.

There is a well-written article I highly advise you to read before reading on You can also access the article with this URL —http://tcat.tc/2u4Klmh — or by searching for, "20 Diversion Tactics Highly Manipulative Narcissists, Sociopaths and psychopaths use to silence you" on ThoughtCatalog.com

Signs of a Toxic Relationship

Unless you have chosen and given your consent to any of these dynamics in your relationship, this type of behavior can be hazardous to your mental and physical well-being.

Consent is not enough; informed consent must always be given.

From the article I mentioned, it seems that there has been much confusion and overlap between the two terms and their diagnoses in the past. Psychologists have generally now started using a single term encompassing both psychopathy and sociopathy: Anti-Social Personality Disorder.

Some of this behavior detailed does fall under the realm of BDSM activity as long as you both have given informed consent, but are signs of abusive behavior if not.

- They're always playing the blame game and never take responsibility for anything.

- Lack of integrity and maturity on their part.

- Their schedule is so full that it leaves no time for you.

- Isolation; your partner is keeping you from family, friends. No activity outside the home.

- Financial control; taking charge of finances, micro-managing your spending habits. (Not always. Many Dom's do take charge of the home finances and many s-types prefer it that way. Again, comes down to preference and consent.)

- The use of violence or threats to maintain a sense of power. This could be a sign of insecurity on their part. Yelling and screaming at someone is not a healthy way to communicate with anyone.

- Stalking you, invading your personal space such as showing up at your workplace unannounced once too often. Checking your phone messages and call logs, e-mails, social media accounts. Stalkers should not be taken likely and should be reported to family, friends, and the police.

- The answer no from you is not an option.

- They constantly treat you more like an object than a person. (In a Master / Mistress slave relationship, s-types are considered property and as long as you have agreed to such a dynamic, it's not considered abuse.)

- Lack of any empathy and concern towards your safety and well-being.

- Jealousy, constant feelings of insecurity that can't be reassured. Pathological, persistently jealous behavior can be quite dangerous and can lead to assault, suicide, and even homicide.

- Constant verbal abuse outside of consensual and mutually enjoyed dirty talk.

- Being taken for granted, not being acknowledged for your commitment to the relationship.

- Issues in the relationship that have not been addressed, despite numerous attempts.

Negotiating the Dynamics of the Relationship

I cannot simply tell you what to include or not to include. I'll explain my own dynamics later on in this book in the "Training 101" chapter. Take and add whatever you desire to incorporate into your own dynamic relationship and journey.

Human Biology

Both Dom and s-type should study and have a basic, fundamental understanding of the human body's nervous system and blood flow. During any bondage scene, keep a close eye on your partner. It's not a good idea to leave them all tied up, alone an unmonitored. Bondage does restrict the flow of blood or pinch nerves and can cause damage to the body in any number of ways. I suggest taking a class in CPR, as well.

Protocols, House Rules and Proper Etiquette

Not everyone in the scene incorporates them. During a scene you may decide to incorporate some protocols, but outside of that it could just be life as you already know it. It just depends on how deep into the rabbit hole you're both willing to go.

Chapter 2:

Training 101

"Responsibility lays on both ends of the leash. Don't ever forget that."

The s-type says. "Why train? I already know most of this." The Dom says. "No, you don't, you just think you do. Now you'll learn how to do things my way."

Like I mention early on in this book, every Dom has their own way, and they have no idea of what you already know or don't know. Remember, we don't own any magical, mind-reading crystals balls.

Is my training method the right way? The wrong way? The only way? **<u>Fuck no!</u>** It's not any of those, and it's definitely not carved in stone. Take, add, and adjust it as you see fit and make that one your very own, the dynamics of which you both agreed to incorporate into your relationship and which will be your very own, custom design.

So, you found your special Dom or s-type, you're both in blissful love heaven, now it's time for the Gates of Hell training, as I personally refer to it. You're both going to be entering this gate together. But why do I call it that? Because it takes a lot of work and dedication from the both of you.

Yes, this takes as much work for the Dom as it does for the s-type. Your Dom will be studying your devotion and willingness to comply and follow his commands, protocols, house rules, and public and private code of etiquette.

Dom's, your s-type will be observing your self-control and ability to stay within their limits, and how devoted you are to their training and this lifestyle. Some s-types can be a bit mischievous, playful, testing you to see if you catch them breaking a house rule or protocols. When you do catch them, take the acceptable, agreed-upon form of punishment that you feel is required to correct this behavior. An s-type can be mischievous and playful while also staying within your protocols and house rules. They may look for loopholes in your training, and some Dom's even encourage this, as the rebellion is part of the fun and helps to relieve stress in their lives and so, in turn, yours. A happy, healthy well-adjusted s-type and Dom will make for a heathy relationship.

Issues will arise, but they will be dealt with like mature adults. The blame game doesn't work, ignoring problems doesn't work. Stepping up and being responsible does. Make whatever necessary adjustments that are required and move on from there. s-types pay attention here, as some Dom's don't care much for brats or S.A.Ms, Smart Ass Masochists. Other Dom's who are just starting out simply don't know how to deal with one or understand their behavior.

My training method is my personal method of educating / training someone, regardless of their life experiences. Every Dominant has their own way on which they run their life and household. This training method is designed for a LTR type of relationship, but pick and choose, add or subtract as you see fit according to your own personal dynamics.

Their way of doing something (this applies to both types) isn't always acceptable. Training bridges those gaps and brings all those dynamics that you both agreed to together.

Missteps and mistakes are going to happen along the way — it's inevitable, we're only human after all. No Dom or s-type is perfect. Make sure there's open honest communication after such an occurrence. If an issue arises, the s-type should always be allowed to speak up without regret, as should the Dom. Writing out the issue is one of the best ways I have found for both parties to express themselves fully and objectively. It helps you pick and choose your words more carefully after you both have calmed down emotionally from whatever ordeal you're dealing with. Again, there are no crystal balls.

The lesson learned by the s-type in this type of relationship is to control their fears through understanding and trust, to be better focused in their everyday life, to create a sense of structure, and to fulfill the s-type's nurturing nature and have a sense of purpose other than themselves in their lives. To correct bad behavior and be a better well-adjusted person. To nurture their emotional needs and not just their sexual erotic desires. To be appreciated by their Dom for their commitment and servitude, and not to be abused or taken for granted.

(Special note here: Some types enjoy being used and viewed as a fuck toy or the like by their Dom, and so they incorporate that dynamic into their lifestyle. See glossary: Objectification; Humiliation; Degradation.)

The Dom should do whatever he feels necessary to build up his s-type's level of confidence and self-esteem and not become abusive towards the s-type. To build mutual trust and respect for one another built on a solid foundation of love, trust, understanding, communication, and mutual respect for one another is the first and last goal of any BDSM type of relationship.

You may wish to incorporate a private opening and closing ceremony once the training period begins and ends. The submissive will be required to present to their Dom a hand-written pledge of her servitude to him, sealed with a kiss, if you like. You may wish to include a pledge of your own.

Training

Before the s-type reaches heaven, they must endure the training period. This will be their Boot Camp Training period. This period will last as long as required, but not longer than needed. Training bridges all the gaps and will put both of you on the same page with each other.

Special Note for Dom's and s-types

For Dom's, keep your training within the limits of your s-type. Age, physical endurance, and any health issues your s-type has will play a role in your training regimen.

The same goes for Dom's, so s-types should keep that in mind. Start with the questionnaire before starting your training. The s-type should create one of their own. Not all Dom's will consent to doing certain things, and neither will s-types. We all have our hard limits, and consent flows in both directions. Everyone involved needs to be on the same page with their kinks and expectations.

Practicing R.A.C.K and S.S.C.

Everything should be open for discussion. The good, the bad, and the ugly, without fear. Communication is the key to a healthy Dom / s-type relationship. The s-type should always be allowed to speak without regret or fear of punishment.

The Dominant and s-type will always make time to discuss any and all issues related to their relationship. Being open and honest with each other is a requirement from both. Being afraid to speak openly will result in failure of the relationship. Feelings of shame, guilt, and fear will be shared between both without being judgmental of each other. Top and bottom dropping are real and require aftercare. Respect and trust are earned, not simply given away.

We all give off red flags and yellow ones, so never discount each other during open communication. Red and yellow flags are real concerns that should be addressed to avoid any confusion or misinterpretations. Too many flags, of course, may mean you're just not compatible for each other. Some of my kinks may not be for you, some of your kinks may not be for me, but mutual kinks can be shared together once trust has been established.

Punishments

No punishment given by the Dominant to the s-type should ever be done when the Dominant is either angry or becomes frustrated. Acting out in anger is not acceptable.

Never punish an s-type for breaking a protocol or house rule they were not made aware of by you. Don't just make up protocols or rules on the fly and expect your s-type to know them. You both may decide to keep a ledger of some sorts to keep track of protocols, house rules, infractions, etc. Some relationships have as many as 500 pages, but use the old-fashioned K.I.S.S. system for starters. Keep It Simple Stupid. It's classic because it works.

Dom's and s-types do get sick from time to time, so during this timeframe, lighten up. Even the toughest just need some soup sometimes.

Bad behavior should never be tolerated. Toxic behavior, mouthing off, not performing duties as needed, laziness, not keeping to a time schedule, breaking protocol or routines such as house cleaning, food shopping, etc. One of my own personal dynamics is to have my s-type thank me as I'm punishing them physically. Spanking them to tears, etc. I have them say, "Thank you, Sir. Thank you for taking the time to correct my bad behavior." Saying it over and over. The submissive should always thank their Dom after being punished. After all, if your Dom didn't care about you, would they take the time to punish you to correct this bad behavior of yours? Hell no.

One of the worst forms of punishments for some s-types, however, isn't physical. It's mental. Simply saying, "I'm not angry with you, I'm disappointed in you." What s-type would feel proud about disappointing their Dom?

Not all punishment needs to be physical. Depending on the infraction, the submissive may be required to stand in the corner facing the wall for a period of time or stand or be tied in some other uncomfortable or humiliating pose. They may be made to perform actions, such as clean the bathroom toilet with a toothbrush, scrub the floors on their hands and knees, pick up rice off the floor one grain at a time, be required to kneel on rice for a period of time, etc. or be asked to perform writing assignments such as "Why are punishments so important?" I don't recommend ignoring your s-type, as you don't want them to feel abandoned (unless they want to feel abandoned over a short time).

If you're the s-type, you will be expected to make rational, logical choices for yourself. Will you expect your Dom to micro-manage your life? Some s-types may just be seeking that much dominance in their life, or they may prefer to keep their day-to-day agency outside the bedroom. A 24/7 situation is often called a TPE, or Total Power Exchange, relationship and may or may not be what you are looking for.

Hard Limits

You'll each need to create a list of your hard limits. The glossary will help you out in this area if you are looking for ideas or are not sure where to start. Other dynamics, such as when family or friends come over to visit or you visit them, etc., can be discussed more in-depth as suits your needs.

A list of any health issues for Dom's and s-types should be made. Medications taken, physical limitations, recent or lingering injuries, etc.

During this training period, keep a close eye on your s-type. Look for signs of being stressed too far. Set aside some time for them to just be themselves.

Nonverbal Communication

It's important that you both are able to communicate with each other during a scene should your s-type be gagged or otherwise unable to speak or signal. Use of a small dinner bell in their hand, shaking their head side to side, dropping an object to the floor, or using hand signals all work quite well. If noise can be made through a gag even if clear words can't be formed.

Bondage Scene

Ropes should always be made of safe, strong materials. Restricting body parts can impair blood flow and cause nerve damage if handled improperly, resulting in injury or even death. You should not attempt any tie on your partner without research, education, and practice. Safety scissors should be kept nearby in case of an emergency. Hemp and jute ropes are best.

Shameless plug alert here. I do sell rope wax on e-bay. Search phrase, natural rope treatment wax.

I personally don't recommend leaving the room during any bondage play, leaving your s-type laying on the floor or on the bed alone or confined elsewhere. Should an s-type ask you to do this, use a child video monitor to keep an eye on them. You can also use Skype. This type of loosely or un-monitored activity is more dangerous than it appears to many, is considered part of a generally more dangerous form of BDSM known as edge play, and should only be attempted by experienced people with informed consent after considerable research.

Face Slapping Tip

During a face slapping scene, it's very important that you use your free hand to support the s-type's head. Simply slapping someone without the necessary support can cause damage to the neck. Avoid hitting the eyes and ears, as well. Light love taps along the jaw line and harder slaps along the cheeks work well.

The Gift

Many people view the s-type's submission to a Dom as a gift. A gift is an act of giving someone a present without any reciprocal actions other than a verbal thank you. When a Dom and s-type do finally accept one another, certain expectations and considerations will be expected from the both of you. Things like Love, Respect, Trust, Wisdom, Guidance, Direction and Commitment. The both of you should expect nothing less from each other.

Dom's, if you start taking your s-type for granted the last thing you might just see is their ass as they walk out the door. Dom's, should your s-type have an issue, talk it out like mature adults. Attempting to Dom your way through or out of it doesn't work, because your s-type will start resenting you. s-types, same goes for you as well. You can't simply pout and expect your Dom to know what you need or stay silent as a scene crosses into being too intense. Communication is the key.

"A bad day for the ego is a good day for the soul."

There are some that have a bit of a self-absorbed, self-entitled attitude.

This often comes from upbringing, being spoon-fed and given much in their life by their parents. They grow up thinking they should get all the things that they feel they deserve in life without having to work for it. Have you ever seen a child throw a temper tantrum?

Have you ever seen an adult throw one? A sure sign of immaturity, you can work on correcting this bad behavior through humiliation, objectification, and degradation of your s-type. Be sure to explain to your s-type the why of it all. The how, well, that's up to you as a Dom to decide.

Chapter 3:

The Questionnaire

Below is how I start my bridging all those gaps I mentioned earlier on. Add to it as you see fit using terms from the glossary or elsewhere. Change, add to it, print it on expensive paper, whatever you like to fit your needs.

Every Dom has his way of doing things and every sub has their own expectations. This questionnaire helps to brings them both together on the same page quickly and easily. The s-type should also have a number of questions for their potential Dom.

The s-type seeking guidance, a mentor, or knowledge is required to answer these questions as honestly as possible. The relationship between a Dom and s-type should be built on honesty and trust and be open to any and all discussion.

Let's take this new beginning one step at a time. Answer the questions below and be as honest with yourself as possible, not holding back out of fear of being judged; shyness will only result in a less-than-expected experience for the both of you. Trust and respect are earned, not simply given away. Life experiences will differ; you need to bridge those gaps together.

1) How much empathy should your potential Dom have towards you?

Answer on a scale of 1 to 10, 10 being the highest. _____

Explain your reason for your level of empathy requirement.

_____

_____

2) How much life experience do you have living the lifestyle?

_____

3) Does the feeling of helplessness and being controlled by another excite you?

Yes_____ No_____ Only during sex _____

4) Does fear and the sense of danger excite you?

Yes_____ No_____.

5) How high would you say is your pain tolerance?
1 being the lowest and 10 the highest. _____

Your idea of, say, a level 5 pain level and my idea of a level 5 would most likely be different. This should be explored slowly during any play activity and always start at level 1 and progress up from there.

6) Are you interested in bondage and domination only?

B & D activity? YES_____NO_____

7) Are you interested in both B&D and S&M activity?
Yes_____ No_____

8) Everything your Dom is about to do must be explained.
Agree_____ Disagree_____ Fuckin' right it does_____

9) Have you ever experienced Bottom dropping?

Yes_____ No_____

Top Dropping? Yes_____ No_____

If yes did your Dom (or s-type) at the time support you during this drop?
Yes_____ No_____

Yes or no, explain how that experience affected you:
_____
_____

10) Has a Dom you were with ever experienced Top dropping? Yes_____ No_____

If you answered yes, then what did you do to support him? Did you lose respect for them? Explain why.
_____
_____
_____

11) The ultimate gift a submissive can give to any Dom is their willingness to give up control and serve their needs. Would you agree? Yes_____ No _____

My submission is a gift. I expect to be treated with dignity, love and respect. I'm not a doormat outside of play. Unless I fully agree to being treated that way, see glossary for my Hard Limits and Soft Limits. Agree _____ Disagree _____

If no, explain.

_____

_____

12) The act of being manipulative / selfish during a play scene is a good thing. Would you agree?

Yes_____ No_____

13) An s-type / Dom is a caregiver of not just sexual or erotic pleasure. Would you agree?

Yes_____ No_____

14) How important is feedback or being vocal during play? Talking dirty, moaning, etc. Scale of 1 to 10, with 10 being the highest. _____

15) How important is aftercare for you?

1 being the lowest, 10 the highest. _____

16) Check off all that apply to you (s-types).

A)

I like it rough_____.

I'm the sensual, sensitive s-type_____.

Little of both _____.

B)

I don't have a lot of experience in BDSM but I am more than willing to learn. I'll take this one step at a time. _____

C)

I have some experience and do know generally what is expected. _____

I am well-versed in BDSM terms, have had multiple experiences, and know my boundaries and interests _____

D)

I can't stop thinking about being the best s-type that I can be. _____

I need and want a Dom to draw it out of me. _____

I'm a bit of a brat and require correction at times. _____

I only want to practice BDSM occasionally or am not sure about my level of interest. _____

Explain_____

_____

17) In a Master/ Mistress slave relationship, a slave is property. Is this the type of relationship you're looking for?

_____

I wish to surrender myself completely to your will and be your slave and serve my Master / Mistress in any way they wish, as long as it's within my limits and I consent to "Consent non-consent".

Yes _____ No_____

Only during a M/s play session and not 24/7.

Yes _____ No_____

I am seeking Bondage and Domination only, no S&M activity. _____

I want it ALL, B&D and S&M_____

Other or don't understand, explain.

_____

18) There are many different kinds of Doms / s-types; how would you describe yourself? *You also can take a FREE BDSM profile test at http://www.bdsmtest.org*

_____

_____

19) How important is physical appearance?

Very_____ Middle ground_____ Don't care _____

20) Check off all that apply to you.

A) I don't care, as long as the Dom satisfies and fulfills my needs as a s-type and appreciates me as a kind, nurturing person. _____

B) The chemistry must be there, physical appearance and age does have some priorities, but if there's chemistry between us — Watch out, I want you! We can learn and grow together. _____

C) I'm not looking for Love, I'm not looking for Mr. Right, I'm looking for Mr. Right Now. Friend with benefits is all I need or want in my life right now. _____

D) I enjoy or entertain the idea of being in a polyamorous or polyfidelity relationship.

I'm looking for a poly partner. _____ No, I'm not poly. _____

(POLYFIDELITY: A closer, more intimate relationship structure where all members are considered equal partners and agree to restrict sexual activity to only other members of the group.)

E) I don't just want the physical; I am also looking for the emotional support as well. _____

F) I want to be in a monogamist relationship _____

21) Relative to your age, health, and experience, how physically strict should your Dom be with you?
On a scale of 1 to 10, 10 being the highest level. _____

22) Do you expect your Dom to micro-manage your life?
Yes_____ NO_____

23) Are you seeking a 24/7 s-type lifestyle?
Yes_____ No_____ Maybe_____
Don't know. _____ I'm a newbie, let's take this slow _____

24) Do you enjoy role playing? Cosplay? What kind?

_____

_____

25) What are some of the worst experiences you ever had? (Why ask this question? You don't want to repeat someone else's mistakes.)

_____

_____

26) What triggers a bad memory in you?

Smells_____

Foods_____

Locations_____

Certain kinds of role play _____

Certain adult toys _____

Bad trigger words you don't like.

_____

27) What triggers a good memory in you?

_____

_____

28) What type of Dom / S-type relationship are you seeking?

Master_____ Mistress_____ Dom_____ Daddy_____
Mommy_____ Other _____

slave _____ submissive _____ little _____
princess _____ Other _____

29) Your initial training period (boot camp for s-types) may be intense. Do you feel up to such a challenge?
Yes _____ No ____ Don't know _____

30) What other books have you read on this subject?

_____

_____

31) What type of porn videos turn you on the most, if any?

_____

_____

32) Who's your favorite porn star, if you have one?

_____

33) Do you enjoy anal sex? Yes _____ No _____
I may be interested in exploring this option later on. _____

34) What kind of impact play do you enjoy most, if any?

_____

_____

None, I'm not a masochist. _____

35) Do you currently have any S.T.Ds? (This question is
not intrusive to anyone asking to be a sexual partner.
Playing safe is a key responsibility.)

Yes_____ No_____

Explain _____

36) Are you currently taking any medication?
Yes _____ No _____

If yes, what kind and for what? Research their side effects.

_____

_____

37) Do you use illegal drugs?
Yes _____No_____ On occasion _____

Weekends only_____ 420 only_____ Other _____

Explain: _____

_____

38) How often do you drink alcohol beverages?
Frequently___ Socially ___ Occasionally___ Never ___

39) Do you have any physical limitations I need to be aware of? If yes, please explain.

_____

_____

40) Have you had any surgery / broken bones in the past five years? If yes, please explain.

_____

_____

_____

_____

41) At the end of the day, we are both human beings, with feelings and emotions.

The play is fun and important but a person's wellbeing always comes first.

Would you agree? Yes_____ No_____
Sometimes _____

42) How many Dom's / s-types have you play partnered with in the past three years?
One ___ Less than 5 ___ More than 5 ___ None ___

43) Answer and explain all that apply below.

Do you live alone? Yes ___ No ___

With parents? Yes ___ No ___

Roommates? Yes ___ No ___

Married in an open relationship. Yes ___ No ___

Currently getting divorced. Yes ___ No ___

Kids living with you _____ Pets _____

Any obsessed, stalking ex-partners?
Yes ___ No ___

If yes, explain the circumstances.

_____

_____

_____

Are you currently married? Yes ___ No ___

Do they know? Yes ___ No ___ If yes, may I contact them? Yes ___ No ___

Are you currently in any type of relationship of any kind?
Yes ___ No ___

If yes, do they know you are here? Yes ___ No ___
If yes, may I contact them? Yes ___ No ___

If you live with your parents, are they obsessed with your every move, overly protective of you? Yes _____ No_____

Any overly protective siblings, friends, or any other family member? Yes _____ No_____

44) Is there any ongoing drama in your life or anything else that I need to be aware of that might negatively affect my life? Yes _____ No_____

If yes, then please explain.

_____

_____

_____

45) Do you know what safe words are for? Yes____ No ___

46) Do you know what your safe words are?
Yes_____ No_____

47) Do you feel safe words should be the only way to stop any ongoing activity?
Yes_____ No _____ Fuck no _____

48) How important is aftercare for you? Scale of 1 to 10, 10 being the highest. _____

49) As a Dom type, do you offer aftercare willingly, or must it be asked for?
Asked for prior to any activity _____Only when needed_____

50) For Dom's, just what is your perception, expectations on this type of relationship? How do you view your life together with an s-type? Add an attachment if needed.

_____

_____

51) For s-types, just what is your perception, expectations on this type of relationship? How do you view your life together with a Dom? Add an attachment if needed.

52) Why do you feel punishments are so important in this dynamic? (For both Dom's and s-types to answer.)

_____

_____

_____

_____

53) Have you ever been diagnosed with a psychological disorder? Yes _____ No_____

If yes, explain.

_____

_____

54) What kind of relationship are you looking for?

Check off what currently applies. This may change over time.
FWB. Friend with benefits_____
 Paly Partner non-sexual _____
LTR. Long term relationship
STR. Short term relationship_____
NSA. No strings attached _____

Chapter 4:

Dom / s-type Contract

Contracts are more of an outlined agreement than an actual contract in a traditional sense; a BDSM contract is not legally binding in any court of law in or outside the United States. It's just something you may wish to incorporate into your relationship as part of your dynamics and as a communication tool to very clearly define limits and parameters to scenes and to the relationship as a whole.

While a contract is certainly not a requirement to any BDSM relationship and they are not legally binding, breaking part of the contract does show a certain lack of spirit for it all, and not having clear guidelines can lead to miscommunication or worse. During the course of your relationship, you may decide to change a few things, add an amendment, expand the boundaries of what you will explore, perhaps, so include only what you are comfortable with in the beginning. Contract terms can be as short or long as you both wish them to be. Have fun with it, change it as you see fit, and play safe.

Mostly, what follows are just a few ideas to get you started. Master / slave, Dominant / submissive, Mistress / slave, Daddy / little, Daddy / princess, Mommy / slave, whatever aspect of the lifestyle you choose to explore is entirely your decision.

Sample BDSM Contract

This is an agreement entered into by
_____ (Dominant) and _____ (s-type).
The purpose of this contract is to state the boundaries in
which this relationship shall function.

Article One; CONTROL

Section One:

The Dominant must have control over his s-type for
a Dominant / s-type relationship to function. The Dominant
must, though, respect that the s-type has an option to say no
but face a consequential punishment instead. The Dominant
will give lead to his s-type to handle daily life and
situations only as he sees fit.

The s-type must realize that only through giving of
themselves to their Dominant can they both be truly happy
and fulfilled in life. The s-type must fully trust
their Dominant completely, freely giving their heart, mind,
and body to their Dominant.

Section Two:

The Dominant must respect the s-type's job or
career and never do anything to risk their livelihood. They
must also respect the s-type's right to privacy and not make
them lose face with family, friends, co-workers, neighbors,
or other social connections without the s-type's consent.

Section Three:

The Dominant and s-type must keep in mind the

spirit of the lifestyle. A loving relationship full of happiness, friendship, and love will be the basis of this relationship. The Dominant/ s-type relationship must stay within the boundaries of this agreement.

Section Four:

The Dominant must not misuse this control in any way by avoiding the Hard Limits that have been pre-agreed upon in Article Three of this contract.

Article Two; PUNISHMENTS

Section One:

The Dominant must exercise the ability to lovingly retain the control that their s-type has freely given over to them. As such, punishments must be in place to deal with the s-type's bad behavior who would decide that their will supersedes that of their Dominant.

Section Two:

Punishments must be at the discretion of the Dominant. However, the Dominant should keep in mind that punishing for the fun of punishing can kill the spirit of the Dominant / s-type relationship. However, s-types should realize that during their basic training period, punishing will be fairly normal as they adjust to the life-style.

The type of punishments given will not be what the s-types enjoys. s-types should keep in mind that not following protocols, house rules, or improper etiquette on a regular basis does kill the spirit of the relationship.

Article Three; HARD LIMITS

Section One:

A Hard Limit is something that BOTH the Dominant and s-type agree will not be on the table to explore or do. *(See attached glossary of BDSM terms in Chapter 5 for Hard Limits, Soft Limits, and Like to Try to clearly outline what's what. For both Dominant and s-type.)*

Section Two:

Safety protocols or related requests are not to be ignored or dismissed. Safety words are words or signals that all parties have agreed to use when necessary. The words "Stop" or "Slow Down" can all be used when starting out. The "traffic light" system or a custom system can be strictly enforced at a later time as the relationship grows.

RED / STOP – All activity stops and the Dominant will check in with the s-type; both will mutually decide to either continue or end the activity.

YELLOW / MERCY / SLOW DOWN – The intensity of the activity both are currently engaged in will slow down but not come to a complete stop. The Dominant may check in from time to time by asking if the s-type is fine.

GREEN / GOOD - Good to go, don't stop!

s-types can use their safe words at any time to stop any play without any regrets from their Dom.

*DOMS — NEVER, EVER PUNISH YOUR S-TYPE FOR USING A SAFE WORD!

Article Four; PUNISHMENT LEVELS

Section One:

It is not in the spirit of the lifestyle to write down all of the punishments that may be given to a s-type for disobedience. Not knowing is often part of the punishment. But there will be three Levels of punishment as listed below.

Level One – Light punishment that could include a basic task that the s-type may not enjoy.

Level Two – Moderate pain with a humiliating task.

Level Three – The greatest punishments.
I'm not angry with you, I'm disappointed in you. Now here's your punishment."

Article Five; Long Term Agreements

Section One:

Pictures and videos. The pictures and videos that are taken by either Dominant or s-type are property of both and consent must be given for uploading to any website or on any social sharing platform.

Article Six; Agreement

This contract / agreement is a formality; it is part of any BDSM play. The Dominant will protect his s-type, love her, cherish her, and the s-type will be the Dominant's best friend.

Dominant _____ Date _____

s-type _____ Date_____

In essence, the Dominant and s-type are now one. By definition, s-types that are collared have agreed to be a part in their Dominant's choice of lifestyle. The Dominant belongs to his s-type through devotion, guidance and discipline.

A kiss from the s-type is required to seal this contract agreement.

Chapter 5:

Glossary

Choose activities that are Hard or Soft Limits.
Choose activities you would most like to try.

The following is a directory of BDSM terms &
SAFE WORDS to be used.

This can be a useful tool for detailing exactly which
activities will be explored throughout your BDSM or D/s
relationship. By signing and dating this document, the Dom
and s-type agree to abide by and acknowledge that both
parties have read and understand all written material in this
section.

Both parties will respect and abide by all agreed
upon safe words and limits.

Both the Dom and s-type are required to read and
mark accordingly. All activities and devices that both
parties have agreed to use or try will be marked with a
green marker. Hard Limits will be marked with a red
marker. Any activity designated as a "Soft Limit" — or
something both parties would like to try with specific
guidelines or precautions — will be marked with a yellow
marker.

Not all definitions require a notation. Many are
simply to expand your knowledge base.

This glossary of BDSM terms should be reviewed from time to time by both the Dominate and s-type together to determine if any changes may be required.

We have both read, agreed to and acknowledge the dynamics and activity set forth in this glossary.

Dominant: _____

Date: _____

submissive: _____

Date: _____

Glossary of BDSM Terms

24/7: Those who live, eat, and breathe this lifestyle 24/7.

A-FRAME: Bondage furniture in the shape of the letter A, similar to a St. Andrew's Cross.

ABASIOPHILIA: Those who incorporate orthopedic fixtures into their BDSM activities.

ABRASION: The use of anything that has a rough surface to it that involves brushing or stroking the skin. A form of sensation play.

ABSOLUTE POWER EXCHANGE: The complete and total exchange of power without question. This type of play may include or disregard safewords, and is thus sometimes considered a form of edge play despite not having direct ties to physical danger. Related to consensual non-consent.

ADULT BABY: A person who enjoys playing the role of an infant or young child in age-play scenarios.

AFTERCARE: After engaging in a very intense BDSM activity, the Dominant cares for and comforts the s-type, reassuring them that they are safe. The Dominant may also relocate the s-type to another room or area where the s-type may feel more safe and secure. It is best to establish an agreed upon no-play area of the house where the s-type can feel safe.

AGE PLAY: The misconception that many people have about age play is that it's a form of or may be related to pedophilia. The truth could not be further from this. It is the sense of helplessness created by the illusion of an age difference that is found so appealing to those who engage in this form of play. A form of role play, adult baby, or infantilism.

AGONOPHILIA: Psychosexual arousal of one who struggles and pretends to resist before being overpowered. Role play could include a rape scene, kidnapping, or home invasion. Also referred to as resistance play.

AGORAPHILIA: Sexual arousal from performing a sex act in public place. Not necessary an exhibitionist. The arousal often comes from the fear of being caught in the act.

ALGOPHILIA: The enjoyment of someone receiving pain, whether observing, dealing or receiving. An umbrella term including masochism, sadism, etc. May be enjoyed by both Dom and s-type's.

ALPHA SUB: When a Dom may have more than one s-type, such as in a polyamorous relationship, one of those s-types may be deemed the "alpha sub," marking them as the most powerful or dominant among the subs. The sub may play a greater role in a domination scene or take the place of the Dominant in his/her absence. Not all such relationships have such a hierarchy.

ANAL BALLHOOK (or BUTT HOOK): A smooth metal rod bent in the shape of a hook, with a metal ball at one end and a metal ring at the other.

ANILINGUS: Oral anal sex. A sexual activity involving licking, kissing, or tonguing another person's anus. Proper hygiene precautions are highly recommended prior to such activity.

ANIMALISM: A form of role play in which one person plays the role of an animal. Pony play, puppy play, kitten play are common forms of animalism.

ANKLE CUFFS: Any restraints that are placed around the ankles.

ARMBINDER: May also be referred to as a single glove or mono glove. A restraint device where both arms are inserted, restraining them together. Used to immobilize your s-type's arms.

ARM TRAPS: A type of restraint designed to go around the elbow and hold the arm in a bent position.

ASPHYXIA: An often misunderstood sexual activity. People practice auto or self-asphyxiation for pleasure. The sense of sexual arousal comes from the lack of oxygen to the brain. Considered by many as one of the most dangerous forms of edge play. Hundreds of people die from this form of edge play every year. **Auto-erotic asphyxiation** is the self-practice of asphyxia for sexual purposes.

ASS PLAY: Any form of sexual activity that involves the anus.

ASYMMETRIC BONDAGE: A bondage technique in which a person is bound in an asymmetric pose.

AUCTION / SLAVE AUCTIONS: Those who agree to have themselves auctioned off to another for a particular scene, such as flogging, spanking, bondage, etc. The scene would be monitored by either their Dom, a friend or a Dungeon Monitor. Dominants may also auction themselves off as well. The auction can take place with fake or play money or may be part of a fund-raising event.

BALL BUSTING: Any activity that involves the testicles, such as squeezing, impact or binding.

BALL GAG: A round ball attached to straps on both ends. The ball is placed within the mouth and the straps are secured around the head used to hold it in place.

BALL HOOD: A type of hood containing air bladders that, when inflated, press against the head, thus closing off the opening for the eyes, ears, or mouth. Used during sensory deprivation play.

BALL PRESS: May also be referred to as a ball crusher.

BALL TIE: Tying a person into the shape of a ball.

BANDAGE SCISSORS: Specialized scissors used by emergency medical personnel to remove bandages. Can also be used to cut ropes and plastic in case of emergencies and are often kept nearby during bondage scenes for safety.

BASTINADO: Any form of impact play that involves the soles of the feet.

BDSM: an acronym for Bondage, Discipline, Sado-masochism.

BEAR'S PAW: A glove with dull metal spikes or hooks on the finger tips.

BELTING: The act of using a leather belt to strike a person.

BERKLEY HORSE: An adjustable type of bondage furniture used to restrain a person in a bent over position, often similar in appearance to a gymnastics pommel horse.

BIRCH: A striking implement comprised of long thin wooden rods.

BLINDFOLD: Anything designed or used to prevent a person from seeing by covering the eyes.

BLOOD PLAY; A type of edge play that includes, but is not limited to, cutting, needle play, knife play. Considered a form of edge play.

BODY BAG: A bag shaped like a sleeping bag, and which may have inflatable bladders to restrict a person movement. Used in some forms of mummification.

BODY HARNESS: A series of leather straps that are worn around the torso. May incorporate metal rings for attaching ropes or chains.

BODY MODIFICATION: Body piercings, tattoos, brandings, and other temporary or permanent changes to one's body.

BODY WORSHIP: Any activity that regards with reverential respect a part of the human body. Foot worship as an example.

BOI: Normally a female with tomboyish or masculine manners or appearance. May often be referred to as a butch.

BOLERO STRAITJACKET: A straightjacket with an opening in the front to expose the breast area.

BONDAGE: The use of any material that restricts a person's movements. Ropes, chains, etc.

BONDAGE BELT: May also be referred to as a Bondage Harness. A device that can be locked into place so the wearer is unable to remove it. May incorporate several attachment points. This device usually is not, but could be, a chastity belt.

BONDAGE BUNNY: Anyone who takes pleasure in being restrained with ropes.

BONDAGE MITTEN: A fingerless glove that can be locked or buckled to prevent the wearer from using their hands.

BONDAGE TAPE: A specifically designed tape that sticks to itself but not skin or clothing.

BOOTBLACKING / BOOT WORSHIP: The care and cleaning, or kissing and licking, of boots. Related to military, uniform play, simple domination and submission, and may be part of leather fetish worship.

BOTTOM: A person who wishes to engage in some form of BDSM activity. May include a temporary power-exchange dynamic. Bottoms don't generally give up their authority as a slave would.

BOTTOM DROP / TOP DROP: The feelings of depression or negative emotions after performing some type of BDSM activity. Feeling guilty, loss of their sense of morality, shame. It is important for the Dom and s-type to comfort and support each other in this time of need. This can happen suddenly or may develop over time. *It is always important for those in a D/s relationship to check in with each other and practice aftercare.*

BOTTOM TOPPING: New or experienced s-types making inappropriate, poorly-timed, or incessant suggestions during play. This is often called "topping from the bottom," and is used to refer to a consistent negative behavior rather than simply a poor choice in timing or procedure. Some consider TFTB to be a sign of manipulation, a sign of an s-type trying to direct the scene regardless of what the dominant or top wants, while some s-types feel this language is used by Doms to abuse boundaries and ignore consent. *Clear communication and boundary-setting is crucial prior to any scene to avoid consent violations, build trust, and enjoy scenes with your partner.*

BOX TIE: A type of bondage where the person grabs both of their elbows and then ropes are used to tie the forearms together.

BRANDING: The use of a branding iron to permanently mark the skin.

BRAT: An s-type who refuses to obey their Dom's commands, or taunts and teases them in order to intentionally provoke a response, usually some form of punishment. Bratty behavior may arise when the s-type is feeling their Dom isn't paying enough attention to them or during the normal course of a scene. Bratty behavior can be perceived as annoying or negative, or may be an integral and positive part of a scene or relationship.

Looking for loopholes in house rules or protocols or open defiance are forms and degrees of bratty behavior. A commonly misunderstood s/ type.

BREAST BONDAGE: Wrapping the breasts tightly using rope and cutting off the blood flow. Another sensation is felt from when the ropes are untied and the blood quickly flows back into the breasts.

BREAST PRESS / BREAST CLAMP: A bondage device used to clamp the breasts.

BREAST TORTURE: Any form of pain play involving the breasts and nipples.

BREATH CONTROL / AUTO EROTIC ASPHYXIATION: Considered by many to be an extreme form of edge play and should never be attempted alone. Done to increase sexual arousal and or sexual climax. I highly recommend seeking out those who personally practice this activity for advice.

BREEDING FETISH / IMPREGNATION FETISH: Not limited to pregnancy but may also be associated with lactation and the physical changes in the human body.

BUCK HAMMER: A medical instrument used to test reflexes or neurological function. A form of sensation play.

BULLWHIP: A single tail whip longer than 5 feet normally made of leather with a rigid handle.

BUKKAKE: The act of ejaculation on a person by two or more men.

BUTT PLUG: A sex toy specifically designed to be inserted into the anus.

BUTTERFLY CHAIR: A chair which contains two horizontal planks to which the legs can be secured, affixed to a pivot such that the legs of the secured person can be spread apart.

CABLE LOOP / CABLE SLAPPER: A striking impact toy consisting of one of one or more coated metal loops with a handle. Coating is often rubber, but can be leather or other material.

CABLE TIE / ZIP TIE: A thin plastic strip that can be locked into a loop, commonly used by electricians.

CANE: A thin, flexible impact toy made from rattan, wood, or polycarbonate.

CARABINER: A device used to connect ropes together with a threaded thumb screw to prevent them from accidently opening up. Commonly used by mountain climbers, this device is used by rope riggers when performing rope suspensions.

CAT O' NINE TAILS: A flogger consisting of 9 tails. May have knots on the ends. The tails come in a wide verity of flexible material from leather to thin chains.

CATHERINE'S WHEEL: A large, upright wheel, 8 to 10 feet in diameter, where the person is attached and can be rotated into any position.

CATHETER: Any thin, flexible tube designed to be inserted into the urethra. Used during medical play.

CILICE: Any garment made to be painful to wear. Used in sensation play. Named after a sackcloth or old garment made from rough, coarse material.

CHASTITY: Disallowing sexual release on a submissive by a dominant.

CHASTITY BELT: A lockable harness device intended to prohibit contact with the genitals.

CHASTITY PIERCING: A lockable body piercing intended to prevent sexual intercourse.

CHEMICAL PLAY: A form of sensation play that involves the use of a mild irritant, such as peppermint oil, menthol, ginger, Tabasco sauce, and the like to create sensation.

CHDW: Acronym. Clueless Horny Dom Wannabe. Pronounced "chud-wah."

CINCHER: A type of corset that is shorter than a full corset.

CINCH KNOT: A type of knot made by passing a rope through a looped opening,

CINCH: A type of bondage in which several windings of rope around limbs or one limb are attached to a fixed object, then cinched through the center. Sometimes referred to as a cinch knot.

CLEAVE GAG: A mouth gag made of cloth, which is placed between the wearers teeth to prevent speech.

CLIT CLIP: A specially designed piece of jewelry that can be affixed to the clitoris to provide constant stimulation.

CLOVER CLAMP: A type of nipple clamp that, when pulled, increases its grip.

COCK AND BALL TORTURE: Acronym CBT; Any activity that involves pain play to the male genitals.

COCK BOARD: Two pieces of wood or metal hinged at one end with a hole in the center so that the penis can be locked in place. A form of cock and ball torture (CBT) or ball play.

COCK BONDAGE: The use of any material — rope, twine, fishing line, etc. — used to tie the penis.

COCK RING: A rubber, plastic, or metal ring placed around the base of the penis, thereby constricting it to prevent the outflow of blood and preventing the penis from becoming flaccid.

CO-DOM: Secondary Dom. A dominant who shares a submissive with another Dominant. May or may not be part of a polyamorous relationship.

CO-submissive: Secondary submissive, sometimes referred to as a "unicorn" due to their perceived popularity and rarity. May or may not be in a polyamorous relationship.

COFFIN / GROPE BOX: Bondage furniture in the shape of a long narrow box, normally made of wood, with holes in it so that others may reach in to perform sensation play with the person inside.

COLLAR: Worn by a submissive as a symbol of their submissive nature and/or ownership. There are a number of different types of collars, including training, posture, and drop collars.

COLLARED: A submissive that has agreed to be with a Dominant either in a long term relationship (LTR) or short-term relationship (STR).

COLLARING CEREMONY: A ceremony that celebrates the commitment between a Dominant and a submissive much like a wedding.

CONSENT: Consent is based on the active willing participation of everyone involved in a particular BDSM activity. Consent is the foundation on which all BDSM activity is based on. Informed consent is the giving of consent with full knowledge of risks of any BDSM activity.

CONSENT TO NON-CONSENT: A relationship in which the submissive knowingly and voluntarily gives up the ability to prevent their dominant from doing whatever he or she desires. Consent to non-consent is generally considered as a form of consent. A component of an Absolute Power Exchange relationship and related to Rape Play. This type of play may include or disregard safewords, and is thus sometimes considered a form of edge play despite not having direct ties to physical danger.

CONTRACTS: A negotiated written agreement between a Dominant and a submissive in which both agree to abide by and explore those BDSM activates both have agreed to engage in. Contracts are not legally enforceable in any court, but are rather a helpful tool in defining the boundaries of the relationship. Contracts are considered a useful way of giving each other informed consent and building trust.

CONTRAPOLAR STIMULATION: Related to any form of stimulation which produces both pleasure and pain sensations simultaneously.

CORPORAL PUNISHMENT: To cause deliberate pain or discomfort in response to correcting undesirable behavior. May include spankings and canings, among numerous other activities with or without devices.

CORSET: A tightly fitted garment that is laced and designed to narrow the waist and lift the breasts. Typically worn to shape a woman's figure, but can be part of crossdressing or similar play.

CORSET COLLAR: A specially designed posture collar that may or may not include rigid inserts, but is laced rather than buckled.

CORSET PIERCING: Body modification, A set of metal rings inserted thru the skin, normally side by side, and then laced with ribbon or other material to resemble a corset.

CORSETRY: The act of wearing a corset, often very tightly in order to modify / shape the human body to a desired look.

CO-TOP: A person who acts together with another Top during a scene.

CRACKER: A short piece of cord or leather on the end of a whip.

CROP / RIDING CROP: A thin, flexible shaft wrapped in leather with a looped handle at one end and a leather flat at the other.

CROSS CUFFS: A type of hand cuff which holds the wrists together in a crossed position.

CROSS-DRESSING: Gratification from wearing clothing generally intended for the opposite sex.

CUCKCAKE: The female that has sex with a cuckqueen's partner. A woman who cuckolds another woman.

CUCKOLD: The husband of an adulterous wife. A cuckold may be aware of the outside relationship or not, and may or may not be part of a cuckoldry fetish. A female equivalent is called a "cuckqueen."

CUCKOLDRY FETISH: When a member of a partnership is sexually aroused by the thought of his or her partner having sex outside their relationship. They may or may not desire for the act to actually take place and may or may not want to be present for the act.

CUCKQUEEN: The female equivalent of a cuckold. A woman who desires her male partner to have sex with another woman.

CUFFS: Any restraint which is used to immobilize a person's wrists and/or ankles.

CUPPING / FIRE CUPPING: Sensation play. The use of glass or plastic cups placed over the skin to vacuum out the air inside. A traditional Chinese medicine (TCM), cupping is done to relive pain, inflammation, increase blood flow, promote relaxation and well-being, and as a type of deep-tissue massage. Fire cupping is performed using glass cups and the use of fire to create a vacuum. A form of sensation play. *When fire cupping, keep a fire extinguisher nearby. NEVER SPRAY A FIRE EXTINGUISHER DIRECTLY ON A PERSON; USE COLD WATER OR SMOTHER THE FLAMES WITH A FIRE RETARDANT BLANCKET.*

D/s: Acronym for Dominance / submission.

DACRYPHILIA; Arousal from seeing someone cry.

DEGRADATION PLAY: Any activity that inflicts misery or shame on a person, often through the use of belittling language or servile acts. Often used as a form of emotional punishment, but not always. Those involved in degradation play are referred to as the "degrader" and the "degradee."

DEVICE BONDAGE: Any type of device or furniture used to immobilize a person.

DEVIL'S FIRE: A branding technique using a pointed needle that has been heated, touching its tip lightly to the surface of the skin. Done to create a specific design. Can be part of sensation play and/or body modification. *Keep a fire extinguisher nearby. NEVER SPRAY A FIRE EXTINGUISHER DIRECTLY ON A PERSON; USE COLD WATER OR SMOTHER THE FLAMES WITH A FIRE RETARDANT BLANCKET.*

DISCIPLINE TRAINING: Any activity in which one person trains another person to act and behave in accordance to their wishes, with their consent to do so. Sometimes, but not always, used to correct bad or undesirable behavior, including hygiene, diet, smoking habits, laziness, etc. This may include a number of other protocols, house rules, codes of conduct, etc.

DOM / sub FRENZY: Term used to describe an overwhelming desire to engage in BDSM that can lead to unwise or hasty choices. Particularly used to describe people who have newly discovered this lifestyle and have little to no experience.

DOLLIFICATION: A type of play in which the submissive dresses up as a living doll and the Dominant plays the role of owner.

DOMINA: A female Dominant.

DOMINANT: A person who takes on the role of power and authority over another in a power exchange relationship.

DOMINATE: To exert physical and psychological control over another person with their consent.

DOM: Acronym for Dominant, can be male or female.

DOMINATRIX: A woman who takes on the role of Dominant in BDSM activities. Often, but not always, refers to a "pro-domme," which is a domina or domme who exchanges her services for money.

DOMME: A female Dominant.

DRAGON'S TAIL: A specific type of whip consisting of a handle wrapped in leather with a single lash. The lash is in a triangle shape, forming a tube towards the end and coming to a flat pointed tip.

DREAD KOOSH FLOGGER: A flogger made from a rope handle tied to several Koosh rubber balls. Koosh rubber balls are children's toys that have rubbery filaments attached to a rubber inner core. Used in light forms of sensation play.

DROP COLLAR: A specific type of collar that descends in the front. Many are quite decorative and are worn on a daily basis by the submissive in some relationships, giving both the Dom and sub a sense of ownership.

DUNGEON: A specifically designed room in the home or a public club set up for BDSM activities.

DUNGEON MONITOR: A person in charge that ensures all participants adhere to safety rules, either at a private play party or in a public BDSM club.

EDGE PLAY: Any activity that involves significant risk of injury or physical harm.

EDGING: The act of bring oneself or another to the point of climax, then denying it. Done to create a higher state of arousal. Part of orgasm control play.

ELECTRIC PONY: A form of electrostimulation. A device in the shape of a saw horse with two copper electrodes running across the top. The submissive straddles themselves just above these, hovering over on their toes and trying to avoid coming into contact to prevent their genitalia from being shocked.

ELECTRICAL PLAY: Any form of electrostimulation. There are a number of specially designed devices for this type of play. Violet wands and Tens units are among the most popular.

ENDORPHINS: Endorphins are among the brain chemicals known as neurotransmitters. Endorphins are released throughout the body in response to stress and pain. There are currently 20 known types produced by the human body. The sense of euphoria created through BDSM is attributed to the release of endorphins. A sudden drop may cause depression, sometimes referred to as sub dropping. Joggers refer to the feeling of endorphines released through their strenuous exercise as a "Runner's High."

ENEMA: The introduction of water or some other liquid into the lower bowels thru the anus. Can be incorporated into a number of types of play.

EVIL STICK: A very thin, strong, flexible rod that causes a sharp pain sensation when struck against the skin. The marks they make may last for days.

EXECUTIONER'S HOOD: A specially designed hood that covers the upper section of the wearer's head but not the mouth.

EXHIBITIONIST: A person who enjoys showing others their body, while engaged in a sexual act or not.

EXHIBITIONISM: A person who receives gratification by knowing others are watching or seeing them, whether engaged in sexual acts or not.

FACESITTING; The act of sitting on one's face. Humiliation play.

FALL: The striking end of any type of whip.

FEAR PLAY: Controlled fear play. Psychological play by creating an atmosphere of fear. The subjects may or may not actually be in any real danger.

FEEDER GAG: A gag mouth-piece that prevents the wearer from closing their mouth, allowing anything to be inserted. An open-mouth gag.

FEMDOM: A dominant female.

FEMINIZATION: The practice of training an s-type male to act, dress and behave like a woman, also referred to as sissification. A form of humiliation play. Associated with cross dressing.

FEMSUIT: A specifically designed body suit that resembles a woman's body.

FETISH: Any item, practice, or apparel that causes arousal in a person.

FIDDLE: A ridged bondage device worn around the neck that both locks the neck and binds the wrist together, worn in front, holding the arms in a bend position.

FIGGING: The act of placing a piece of carved ginger root into the anus, creating a burning sensation. A form of punishment or pleasure for some. Dates back to Roman times, when a slave owner felt that their slave was lazy or behaving badly. Also used in the past during horseracing, but is outlawed in modern times.

FIRE PLAY: Any activity that involves fire, such as fire cupping. The use of using lit fire sticks used gracefully and lightly glazing it anywhere along the body. A form of sensation play. *Not for the inexperienced player. Should not be performed around any flammable material. Be sure to have a clear, open space around you. Keep a fire extinguisher nearby. NEVER SPRAY A FIRE EXTINGUISHER DIRECTLY ON A PERSON; USE COLD WATER OR SMOTHER THE FLAMES WITH A FIRE RETARDANT BLANCKET.*

FIRE WHIP / FLOGGER: A single tail whip with a Kevlar tip. Flogger with falls made of Kevlar. Part of sensation and pain play. Should be performed outdoors only. *Not for the inexperienced player. Should not be performed around any flammable material. Be sure to have a clear, open space around you. Keep a fire extinguisher nearby. NEVER SPRAY A FIRE EXTINGUISHER*

DIRECTLY ON A PERSON; USE COLD WATER OR SMOTHER THE
FLAMES WITH A FIRE RETARDANT BLANCKET.

FIRST GIRL: Primary s-type in a triad or other poly relationship. Has a higher status than others and is considered the "primary" relationship.

FISTCUFFS: Lockable padded bondage hand mitts. Used to prevent the wearer from using their hands, fingers.

FISTING: The word is a bit misleading to the inexperienced, as fisting is generally done by bringing the fingers together and slowly inserting them into the vigina. A more intense orgasm is reported for many who enjoy fisting. Can also be incorporated with the anus.

FLAGELLATION: Generic term for any activity involving flogging or whipping.

FLAGGING: Publicly wearing a specific piece of clothing, jewelry, insignia, or color code system showing interest in BDSM activity. See: Hanky Color Code.

FLOG: To strike someone with a flogger.

FLOGGER: A striking implement used in impact play. Has a handle anywhere from 6 to 12 inches long with multiple falls, lashes. Made from leather to chains and anything in between.

FLORENTINE: A stylish flamboyant technique use of floggers typically swung in a figure 8 pattern.

FORCED ORGASM: A form of resistance play forcing a person to engage in multiple orgasms against their will. May include bondage with a sexual stimulation device, such as a vibrator.

FORNIPHILIA: Bondage in combination with objectification. Tying a person and then using them as a piece of furniture, such as a foot stool, table, or coat rack.

FOUNTAIN OF VENUS: Slang term for watersports; being urinated on by a woman.

FREEPLAY: Activities being performed without any domination or submission.

FROG TIE: A specific bondage position where a person kneels and their ankles are tied to the thighs, preventing them from standing up.

FUCKING MACHINE: Any specially designed machine where a dildo is attached to a reciprocating shaft that is attached to a cam wheel and driven by an electric motor. Many have adjustable speed controls.

FUNNEL GAG: A funnel with a long tube attached to it where the opposite end is attached to any open-mouth type of gag.

FURRIES: Term used to describe a wide range of enthusiasts who give anthropomorphic qualities to animals and often portray themselves as animals, sometimes while wearing "fursuits," which are full-body costumes designed to look like animals. Furry activities may or may not be sexual in nature and may or may not be part of pet-play or BDSM at all, but may instead be described as a part of a person's identity.

GAG: Any object that is placed in the mouth, often restricting the person's ability to speak or make noise. There are dozens of types of gags with different functions, some but not all of which are detailed in their own glossary entries.

GENITORTURE: Any specific type of pain play that involves the genitals.

GIMP: A submissive gay male wearing tight fetish clothing with a hood. See: Gimp Hood. Done to ridicule and mock the wearer. A form of humiliation and degradation play.

GIMP HOOD: A hood that completely covers a person's head and face often without any openings for the eyes, nose, ears, or mouth. May be used in degradation play, hostage play, kidnapping play, rape play, etc.

GIMP SUIT: A one-piece, tight-fitting full-body suit that incorporates a gimp hood.

GOLDEN SHOWER: The act of urinating on a person.

GOKKUN: The act of drinking a large amount of semen from a container.

GOREAN D/S: The formal relationship system adapted from the fictitious society described in the Gor novels by John Norman.

GREEK SEX: Slang term for anal sex. Sometimes used in the context of something simply being "Greek."

GWENDOLINE HOOD / SWEET GWENDOLINE HOOD: A hood that covers the entire head and mouth with a large opening for the eyes and nose. Named for a comic character written by artist John Willie in the 1950s and 1960s.

GYNARCHY: A system in which all women are deemed superior to men. A femdom society. Opposite of patriarchy.

HAIR TIE / HAIR BONDAGE: Anything that can be used to tie the hair, then tied to a point to limit a person's head movement.

HANDCUFFS: Any device that is used to restrict a person's ability to use their hands. Normally placed around the wrists. Used by law enforcement and security personnel around the world.

HANKY COLOR CODE: A covert system to advertise the type of BDSM activity one enjoys, with those seeking an activity wearing the color on their left arm and those offering an activity wearing the color on their right arm. Derived from a series of handkerchiefs used by gay men to communicate with each other secretly.

- Black – S&M
- Dark Blue – Anal sex
- Light Blue – Oral sex
- Brown – Scat
- Green – Hustler (Prostitution)
- Gray – Bondage
- Orange – Anything goes
- Purple – Piercings
- Red – Fisting
- Yellow – Watersports

HARD LIMIT: Any BDSM activity a person wishes not to engage in. Having a hard limit crossed is considered a consent violation and is to be avoided. It is best practice to clearly communicate hard limits and for all parties to respect and honor those limits.

HEAD HARNESS GAG: A mouth gag with additional straps that restrict the movement of the head.

HEDGEHOG: A device similar to a rolling pin that has protruding spikes, which is rolled along a person's skin. A form of sensation play.

HOBBLE SKIRT: A very tight-fitting skirt that ends below the knees preventing the wearer from having full motion of their legs. Forces the wearer to walk slowly.

HOBBLE STOCK: Any specifically designed device used to restrain a person by the genitals.

HOG SLAPPER: Impact play item generally made of thick leather or rubber. May be wrapped in a coarse material.

HOGTIE: A specific type of bondage position in which the person laying on their stomach has their wrists and ankles tied to each other behind their back.

HONOR BONDAGE: Sometimes referred to as positioning training. Placing the submissive in a particular position without the use of any restraints. Also referred to as psychological bondage.

HOJŌJUTSU: The traditional Japanese martial art of restraining a person using cord or rope during the medieval times in Japan on prisoners. Shibari is an offshoot of this type of bondage.

HOOD: Any specifically designed device used to cover the head and face. May include opening for the eyes, nose, ears, and mouth.

HORSE: In carpentry, this form is referred to as a saw horse. The form may be covered with leather or rubber, so a person may be bound to it for any number of BDSM activities.

HOUSE BOY: A submissive male house servant that may be utilized in a number of other ways outside of any BDSM activity. Doing common household chores, etc. A domestic. A typically young, male version of a Stepford Wife. May or may not live with their Dominant or be collared by or married to them. While in the home, the submissive may be required to wear fetish clothing or be completely naked.

HOUSE GIRL: A submissive female housed servant that may be utilized in a number of other ways outside of any BDSM activity. Doing common household chores, etc. A domestic. A Stepford Wife. May or may not live with their Dominant or be collared by or married to them. While in the home, the submissive may be required to wear fetish clothing or be completely naked.

HOUSE SLAVE: Much the same as a house boy/girl but does live with their Dominant, is either collared by or married to their Dominant, and in a slave relationship with them.

HUMBLER: A restraining device that fits around the testicles, connected by straps that wrap behind the buttocks and forcing the wearer to walk in a slightly bent over position or on all-fours.

HUMILIATION PLAY: To hold one in contempt by humiliating them, often through degrading language or forced acts. Sometimes incorporates sissification or forced feminization. Not necessarily done for sexual arousal, but done as a power play. This type of play may have little to no risk of physical injury, but can be very psychologically intense. Considered a form of edge play.

IMPACT PLAY: Any activity involving striking a person with anything. Whipping, flogging, spanking, caning, and even kitchen implements or other household objects could be used. While creativity is encouraged, it is best to think out and plan what objects are safe beforehand.

IMPALEMENT: This type of play involves having your partner tied and bound in a position where the anus or vigina are easily accessible and then penetrating them with a dildo attached to a long or short rod or stick.

INFANTILISM: A specific kind of roleplay and part of ageplay. An adult who plays the part of an infant. Wears diapers, a baby bonnet, diapers, pacifier and, in some cases, an adult size baby crib.

INFIBULATION / CHASTITY PIERCING: In women, the sewing of the labia lips closed to prevent penetration and/or removal of the clitoris. In men, the sewing of the foreskin to prevent the male from impregnating a woman. Practiced mainly within religious cultures, but has been adapted by some within the BDSM community, often not to such extremes.

INFLATION: The act of injecting a saline solution into the scrotal sac in order to artificially inflate them. Should only be performed by a skilled, well-experienced person due to the significant medical risks involved. Sometimes also referred to as "salinization" after the saline solution used.

INFORMED CONSENT: General consent is not enough to validate any activity with anyone involved. Informed consent is the act of informing someone, giving them full knowledge of and any of the risks involved including the circumstances surrounding the activity. Informed consent is one of the foundations of any BDSM relationship.

INVERSION TABLE: A bondage piece of furniture where a person can bound to the table and then tilted or rotated in a number of different ways.

IRISH 8 HANDCUFFS: A ridged set of handcuffs in the shape of the number 8. Modeled after a design popular in Ireland.

ISOLATION HOOD: Any hood that prevents the wearer seeing, hearing, or speaking. Used as part of sensory deprivation play.

KARADA: A decorative, yet functional body tie in the shape of multiple diamonds interwoven worn around the torso and legs.

KENNEL PLAY / PUPPY PLAY: A specific form of play where a person acts and behaves as a puppy or dog. May include a doghouse, dog feeding / water dish. Clothing, dog mask or hood.

KINK SHAMING: Undue judgment of someone else's kink or kinks and the vocalizing of that judgment. Considered a faux pas, rude, even abusive behavior by those in the community.

KNEELING STOCK: A ridged piece of bondage equipment where a person can be placed and locked in a kneeling position. The neck and wrists are locked in place.

KNIFE PLAY: Any activity involving use of a sharp or dull knife. Can also be used as part of psychological and fear play. Considered to be edge play due to the risk.

KNOUT: A whip with multiple lashes of leather wrapped with metal wire.

LABIA SPREADER: A device with clamps that are used to hold the labia apart, giving hands-free access to the vagina. Incorporated in humiliation play.

LACING / OBJECTIVATION TABLE: A table or any horizonal surface with eye hooks used to bind a person in a specific position.

LASH: A single length of leather or cord used to strike a person. Impact play.

LEG IRONS: A specifically designed set of ankle cuffs connected by a chain. Allows a person to walk, but not run. Limits leg movements. A form of bondage.

LEG SPREADER: A bar with ankle cuffs that forces the wearer to spread their legs apart.

LIFESTYLE: Referring to the D/s lifestyle, or simply "the lifestyle" in conversation. Of or pertaining to a BDSM lifestyle.

LIMIT: A limit which is set by and agreed to by both Dominant and submissive. There are both hard limits and soft limits, depending on the level of relative discomfort a person has with each activity, with hard limits never to be crossed and soft limits to be carefully and selectively approached over time. The use of safety words and non-verbal signals, such as ringing a hand-held bell, etc., can indicate when a limit has been reached or crossed.

LITTLE / AGE PLAY: Not necessary role play, but can be a way one identifies themselves as. One who takes on the role of someone younger than they are.

MANACLES: Metal hand and ankle cuffs attached to one another with a chain that limits movement.

MARTYMACHLIA: Martymachlia is a fetish that involves arousal stemming from others watching their sexual activity. A specific form of exhibitionism,.

MASOCHIST: A person who experiences excitement, arousal, or sexual gratification from receiving pain specifically applied to various parts of the human body.

MASTER: A Dominant male normally in a Total Power Exchange relationship with one or more submissive. Some females also use the title Master, but more commonly a female Dominant uses the title of Mistress.

MEDICAL PLAY: Any roleplay centering around doctors or a medical setting. Can involve costumes and roleplay, and may also include the use of actual medical devices. See: Catheter, Sounding, Speculum.

METAFETISHIST: A person who enjoys exploring the many facets that BDSM has to offer.

MILITARY PLAY: A type of play involving military-style fetish clothing. 2). A very well-structured, ordered way of living one's life. Many people in a TPE relationship live a well-structured lifestyle with protocols and rules, but do not necessarily involve military play.

MISTRESS: Female equivalent of a Master.

MOUSETRAP: A metal cage used in close confinement of a person. Normally kneeling or on all fours. Body shaped.

MOUTH / HORSE BIT: A cylinder-shaped bit with straps at both ends that can be strapped, locked, or buckled around the back of the head. Used during pony or horse play.

MOUTH GAG: Standard dental instrument designed to hold the mouth open for long periods of time.

MOUTH PLUG: A gag that is used to keep the mouth open, featuring a large opening in the center. Made of rubber or plastic. Some models come with a plug to prevent speech.

MUMMIFICATION: A type of bondage where a person is completely wrapped in plastic or other material: shipping wrapper, Saran Wrap, cloth, rope, etc. To be completely immobilized.

MUNCH: An informal social gathering of like-minded people with a wide variety of interest in BDSM. Unlike a play party, no actual BDSM activities take place at a munch. Usually set in a public place, such as a dinner, café, bar. A safe and low-key event to introduce oneself to the scene and build connections. *Check the events tab on Fetlife.com for local Munches in your area or seek other ways to discover local events.*

MUZZLE GAG: A gag fastened around the head with buckles and straps, which covers the lower part of the face.

NEEDLE PLAY: Any activity involving the insertion of needles through the upper layers of the skin. Considered edge play.

NEWBIE: Someone who is new to the community of BDSM lifestyle.

NIPPLE CLAMP: Any clamp to be used on the nipples of a person.

NOSE HOOK: A blunt hook inserted into the nostrils and tied over the head to prevent the wearer from lowering their head.

NOSE SHACKLE: Any specifically designed clamp used to clamp onto a person's nose with a chain attached to it so as to be able to lead the person about. A form of humiliation play.

OBJECTIFICATION: Any act that dehumanizes another, literally treating them as an object or less than human. Can be a form of humiliation play. A broad fetish, one example of which is forniphilia.

ONE-COLUMN TIE: Any appendage of the human body that is attached to a single, fixed point.

ORAL SERVITUDE: A specific relationship where the submissive serves the Dominant orally only.

ORGASM CONTROL / ORGASM DENIAL: A practice where the dominant takes control over their submissive, denying them orgasms for a period of time or forcing them to have multiple ones.
2). Also referred to as edging when orgasm is denied during sexual activity.

ORIENTATION PLAY: Ordering / instructing a person to engage in a sexual activity within one's own sex. Example: Instructing your submissive female to engage sexually with another female.

OTK: Acronym for Over the Knee.

OVER THE KNEE: The act of taking your submissive and bending them over your knees in order to spank them on their rear end.

OVERSEER'S WHIP: A single-tail whip without a ridged handle.

PADDLE: A stiff, hard, flat implement used for striking a person on the butt.

PAIN PLAY: Any activity, done only with consent, in which one person inflicts pain on another.

PAIN SLUT: A person who enjoys a wide variety of pain play activities that involve a large amount of pain.

PANIC SNAP: A quick-release snap that can be released even under pressure. Used for safety reasons during certain scenes in suspension and bondage play.

PANSEXUAL: A person who engages in sexual or erotic activities with all sexes and orientations.

PARACHUTE: A leather cone that is wrapped around the scrotum, often with suspending weights tied to them to compress the testicles. Used in CBT play.

PEGGING: The act of a woman using a strap on dildo on a man's anus.

PERCUSSION: A type of impact play that involves using a blunt or heavy implement.

PERVERTIBLE: Any ordinary object that can be incorporated into any form of BDSM activity. Examples: Using a cooking pan as a paddle or a clean sock as a gag.

PET PLAY: An activity in which one or more human participants takes on the role of a pet: dog, cat, etc. Not to be confused with bestiality. Pet players may or may not consider themselves furries and may or may not engage in sexual acts during pet play.

PILLORY BED: A bed with built-in head and wrists stock.

PLAY PARTY: A social gathering place in which people participate in BDSM activities.

PLAY PIERCING: Needle play. A form of edge play where needles are passed through the skin.

POLYAMORY: The practice of or desire for relationships with more than one partner with the knowledge of all partners. Consensual, ethical, and responsible non-monogamy.

POLYFIDELITY: A closer, more intimate polyamorous relationship structure where all members are considered equal partners and agree to restrict sexual activity to only other members of the group.

PONY PLAY: A type of roleplay where the submissive plays the role of a pony. Walking on all fours, wearing a mouth bit, and pulling a cart are some examples of pony play. Falls under the umbrella of pet play.

POSTURE COLLAR: A specifically designed ridged collar often made of leather that forces the wearer to hold their head up high.

POWER EXCHANGE: A consensual and voluntary agreement between two or more people where one takes on the role of a

Dominant and the other the role of the submissive. The submissive willingly yields to the authority of the Dominant. This dynamic can be long-term, referred to as a T.P.E, or it can be a short-term, temporary exchange of authority.

PREDICAMENT BONDAGE: Thought of as challenge bondage, where a person is bound loosely but in a way that restricts their movement to a certain degree. This person is then asked to perform general household duties or a sexual act. This can also be incorporated in any number of ways with pain play or other D/s play.

PRO DOMME: A female Dominant that charges a fee for her services.

PROTOCOL: Any designed and enforced code of conduct that a submissive is expected to abide by.

PSYCHOLOGICAL BONDAGE: Bondage without the use of any restraints. The Dominant may command the submissive to take a certain position and not move from that position. Some Dominants impose position training in their dynamics. Also referred to as honor bondage.

PUNISHMENT TIE: Any form of bondage that causes pain or discomfort to a person.

PUPPY PLAY: Any activity in which the submissive takes on the role of a puppy. Barking, walking on all fours, and fetching a stick are examples of puppy play activities. Also includes Kennel play, and is under the umbrella of pet play.

QUEENING: Anilingus. The act of performing oral sex around the anus of another. The nerve endings around the anus are highly sensitive to touch and licking.

QUEENING STOOL: A small 3- or 4-legged stool with a large hole in the center. The submissive is put in position laying on the floor facing up, while the Dominant places the stool over the head of the submissive so as to have access to the anus of the Dominant.

R.A.C.K: Acronym for "Risk Aware Consensual Kink." The concept behind risk aware consensual kink is the acknowledgement of the fact that some BDSM activities may involve a certain level of risk of injury, and that as long as all the participants are aware of any risk and have consented to the activity, the activity is considered ethical.

RACK: Non-Acronym. Bondage furniture. A Medieval implement consisting of a platform and a wheeled mechanism designed to stretch a person bound to it.

RAPE PLAY / RAPE FANTASY: Where participants stage a mock rape scene, often staged so as to fulfill a person's sexual fantasies of rape or coerced sex in a safe and controlled way. Rape play may often push boundaries or may or may not feature the ignoring of safe words during the scene itself, and is thus considered edge play and falls under the umbrella of consensual non-consent.

RESISTANCE PLAY: Any agreed-to activity that involves one person struggling against another in order to subdue them.

RETIFISM: A shoe fetish.

RIGGER: A person who specializes in art of tying up another using elaborate, often creative decorative ties as a form of creative physical expression. Generally, riggers practice the art of suspension. See: Suspension.

RIMMING / RIM JOB: A slang term for Anilingus.

ROLE PLAY / COSPLAY / ACTING: Any activity in which people involved act out a scene in identities not their own. Teacher, student, police or law officer in interrogation play, and so on. Often, but not necessarily ending in a sexual encounter. Cosplay is the dressing up or costuming of oneself after a specific fictional character from pop culture, and is usually not, but can be, done in a sexual setting.

ROPE CUFF: Any form of rope bindings that involve the wrists or ankles together.

ROPE GAG: May have a large knot incorporated in the center and placed in the mouth and tied around the back of the head.

SADIST: A person who derives pleasure, especially sexual gratification, from inflicting pain or humiliation on another. A sadist doesn't necessarily take pleasure in inflicting pain on anyone without their consent, as the pleasure often comes from knowing that the masochist is also enjoying the experience.

SADOMASOCHISM: Any activity that involves the inflicting or receiving pain or humiliation.

SAFE CALL: When meeting someone new, a safe call is the setting up a prearranged phone call with a third party (a friend or someone trusted) that includes a safe or not safe word or phrase. The safe word or phrase should be prearranged and clearly understood by both people so that the signal can be communicated secretly, in case the dangerous person is present during the phone call. This will allow the third party to intervene or otherwise send help without notifying the dangerous person.

SAFE, SANE, AND CONSENSUAL (SSC): An ethical and moral code of conduct which holds that any activity between consenting adults is acceptable as long as they feel it falls within their own mutual guidelines of what's considered safe, sane, and consensual. Subjective to each induvial ideal on what they consider to be safe and sane. Related to R.A.C.K. Edge play is also a related term, but edge play explicitly pushes the boundaries of SSC.

SAFEWORD: Mutually agreed-upon safe words that would slow down or completely stop any BDSM activity. The universally-used safe words are referred to as the stop light code. RED is a safeword which means all activity should stop immediately, YELLOW means "please slow down but don't stop," and GREEN means still good to go, used after a Dom checks in. Some people also use MERCY to slow things down, similar to YELLOW.

SCARIFICATION: Involves scratching, etching, burning / branding. An ancient form of body modification. It's becoming more popular as tattooing and body piercing become more acceptable in today's modern society. Often done in intricate or elaborate patterns.

SCAT / SCANT PLAY: Any activity involving feces / shit. Considered edge play. Feces, unlike urine, is not sterile and so scat play involves the possibility of disease or infection and should be practiced safely. Actual consumption of scat should not be considered due to the high risk factors, and contact with the mouth or mucas membranes should be avoided. Scat play should not be considered when one or more partners is experiencing illness.

SCENE: 1. Any activity where two or more people are or were engaged in D/s behavior. It is considered bad etiquette to disturb anyone during a public scene. 2. Used as a way of describing the BDSM community as a whole, for example, "Are you in the scene?" Similar in usage to "the lifestyle."

SELF-BONDAGE: The practice of tying yourself up.

SEGUFIX / BONDAGE: A medical restraint system, designed to secure a person.

SENSATION PLAY: Any physical activity involving creating unusual sensations on a person's skin. Rubbing ice cubes over various body parts, soft fur, coarse material, etc. Blindfolding your partner, or engaging in other forms of sensory deprivation during sensation play, can heighten these sensations.

SENSORY DEPRIVATION: Used to create a psychological state of arousal or fear or as part of sensation play. Limiting a person's ability to see or hear. Can also be used as part of fear play.

SERVICE D/S RELATIONSHIPS: This type of relationship is centered around the s-type serving the Dominant in practical ways, such as cooking, cleaning, or serving them food. These simple acts taken for granted by many can be a powerful symbol for the submissive and a source of pride as they develop their ability to service and please.

SERVICE TOP: A Dominant who enjoys servicing an s-type or who otherwise engages in servicing activities.

SESSION: This word, in place of "scene," is most often used by pro dommes and mistresses.

SHIBARI / KINBAKU: A type of artful artistic bondage originating in Japan often done with elaborate and intricate patterns. Shibari and Kinbaku are often used to describe the same thing.

SHINJU: A type of rope chest harness that does not restrict motion and can be worn under clothing.

SHOE FETISHISM: A type of expression centered around a fixation on shoes.

SINGLETAIL: A type of whip with a single lash; considered edge play. Skill and training are necessary to proper use, as serious damage can be inflicted by inexperienced people using such a device.

SISSY / SISSIFICATION: An s-type male undergoing feminization training. An s-type forced to wear women's clothing and/or engage in typically feminine behavior.

SLAVE: An s-type in a Total Power Exchange (TPE) relationship with a Dominant. This type of relationship can impact every aspect of their lives, 24/7.

SLAPPER: Two wide leather straps bound together at the handle. Used in impact play.

SLING / SEX SWING: Any flexible material that is suspended from the ceiling or a beam and allows easy access for any sexual activity.

SMOTHERBOX: A tight-fitting, padded head box that may be lockable. The box is placed on the floor and an s-type places his head inside to perform queening, or anilingus, on the Dominant.

SOFT LIMIT: Any BDSM activity that causes a person particular concern due to any number of reasons or circumstances. Typically, soft limits are activities which the person will only engage in under certain conditions, but which are nonetheless not hard limits. A soft limit is typically something that a person is interested in but cautious about, and so engaging in these activities typically requires more than the normal amount of communication, checking in, and aftercare.

SOMNOPHILIA: Engaging in a sexual act with a sleeping person.

SOUND or SOUNDING: A sound is a thin, solid metal rod designed to be inserted in the urethra. Sounding is the act of inserting such a device. Part of medical play.

SPANKING BENCH: A piece of BDSM furniture with a kneeling a platform used for spanking or any other type of impact play.

SPANKING GLOVE: A glove made of either heavy leather or rubber to protect the wearers' hand during spanking.

SPECULUM: A medical device consisting of two or more mechanically spreadable probes. Part of medical play.

SPENCER PADDLE: An oblong wooden paddle 18 to 22 inches long. Some may have holes drilled through them.

SPREADER BAR: A bar 3 to 4 feet or longer with attachments points at both ends. Used to keep a person's legs or arms apart. May also have an attachment point in the center. Restraining equipment used in bondage play.

SQUICK: Word describing the emotional reaction to the idea of any BDSM activity which does not appeal to someone. Disgust or revulsion.

ST. ANDREW'S CROSS: A piece of BDSM furniture commonly 8 feet tall in the shape of an X, used in impact play. Named after a martyred Christian saint whom it was used on, this cross that was an actual ancient torture device is now used as a popular BDSM staple.

STEEL BONDAGE: Any bondage equipment made of steel. Hand cuffs, leg shackles, steel cage. Etc.

STING: Any sharp pain caused by any form of BDSM play, distinct from throbbing or other forms of pain. Part of sensation play.

STOCK: A piece of BDSM bondage equipment used to hold a person's head and wrists between two wooden boards that forces a person to stand hunched over. Part of bondage or humiliation play. Once used as a medieval torture and punishment device, wherein criminals would be placed in public stocks.

STRAITJACKET: A heavy jacket made of canvas where the sleeves end in long straps used to wrap around a person, restricting their arm movements.

STRAP-ON: A dildo attached to a harness designed to be worn around the waist. See: Pegging.

STRAPPADO BONDAGE: A specific type of bondage position in which a person's hands are tied behind the back, then a rope is tied to the wrists and attached to an overhead fixture or pulley tightly enough so that the bound person is forced to bend over with their arms in the air.

SUBMISSIVE: A person who takes on the role of a submissive or has submissive tendencies in their personality. Someone willing to conform or submit to the authority of another in a power exchange relationship. Many submissives don't act or behave submissively in public, and may hold a position of power and authority outside the home. Related to being a switch and/or bottom.

SUBSPACE: A specific state of mind that a person enters, particularly after an intense session / scene. Described as a feeling of blissfulness, a strong sense of well-being. Related to the release of endorphins in the brain. This feeling can last for hours or even days.

SUSPENSION: A form of bondage play where the person bound is suspended partially or completely off the floor. Often done artfully as a form of expression. Many professional riggers often incorporate elaborate artistic poses using rope.

SUSPENSION BAR: A bar made of metal, wood, or bamboo with tie points at both ends and one in the center, often tied to a pully system or electric host so that the person bound to it can be easily raised or lowered.

SUSPENSION CUFFS: Any restraint that is able to distribute the wearer's weight and used in suspension play.

SUSPENSION FRAME: Any ridged, structured frame used in suspension play. Often features tie points to prevent a person from falling off.

SUTURING: The act of temporarily sewing parts of the body together, often done to the genitals. A form of needle play, lacing.

SWITCH: In a BDSM context, a person who switches roles between Dominant and submissive, or a person displaying both Dominant and submissive tendencies.

SWINGER: A person who enjoys sexual relations with others and not necessarily with complete strangers. Some married and dating couples switch partners. See: Polyamorous.

SYBIAN or SYBIAN SADDLE: A type of fucking machine. A dome shaped saddle with a dildo or clitoral attachment with adjustable speed control for its vibrations.

TACK BRA or TACK PATCH: A bra where thumb tacks have been inserted facing the skin, causing constant sensation. Many people use a patch of leather with inserted tacks which is placed inside the bra facing the skin, called a Tack Patch.

TAYLOR HAMMER: A medical device consisting of a triangular rubber hammer attached to a metal handle. Part of percussion play.

TAWSE: A thick, heavy, leather strap that splits off into 2 or 3 ends at the striking point.

TELEDILDONICS: Any specifically designed sex toy designed to be operated remotely, as by wireless remote, a computer network, and so on.

TENS UNIT: TENS, or Transcutaneous Electrical Nerve Stimulation. An electrical device which applies electrical signals through pads affixed to the skin. Used in the medical community as a form of pain management. Tens units have a wide range of settings, from mild to intense. Further research should be conducted in this area should you decide to engage in this form of BDSM. Part of electric or electricity play.

THUD: Any specifically designed heavy-impact play item. A heavy leather flogger, for example.

TOP: A Dominant who administers some form of sensation on a submissive but is not that submissive's partner. May include a temporary power exchange dynamic during a scene. Example: "At the club the other night I negotiated with 2 s-types that consented to bottom for me for a spanking scene."

TIGHTLACER: One who practices the art of lacing.

TOTAL POWER EXCHANGE (TPE): A relationship in which one person surrenders control to another person for an indefinite or short-term duration, and in which the relationship is defined by the fact that one person is always dominant and the other is always submissive.

TRAINING COLLAR: Similar in some ways to an engagement ring in a wedding.

TRAMPLING: A practice in which one person lies on the floor and enjoys being stepped or walked on by another.

TRANSVESTITE: One who enjoys cross dressing. This term has fallen out of use and is sometimes considered offensive, but is not necessarily so. Not to be confused with transgender.

TWEEZER CLAMPS: A type of nipple clamp.

TWO-COLUMN TIE: Bondage. Any two parts of the body tied to each other.

UGOL'S LAW: States that no matter how strange one of your kinks or fetish may be, there's always going to others who share it as well.

UNIFORM PLAY: Role play. Those who find uniforms, particularly uniforms that convey rank or indicate hierarchy or authority, arousing.

URTICATION: Sensation play. The sensation of having been stung by nettles. Related to acupuncture, needle play.

UTILITY D/S: Part of objectification play or service domination. For those involved in utility D/s, sexual submission may or may not be a part of the relationship.

UTILITY GAG: A specific type of gag with a special attachment point for various types of accessories, such as feather dusters, drink serving tray, ash trays, and so on. Part of humiliation play or forniphilia.

VAGINAL HOOK: Similar to an anal hook, only inserted into the vagina instead.

VAMPIRE GLOVES: A glove with needles or sharp pointed protruding from the palms and/or fingers. Part of sensation play.

VANILLA: A person who has no involvement or interest in any or all BDSM activity. May be used as an insult towards someone or a matter-of-fact descriptor of preference, depending on context.

VETO: A polyamorous relationship agreement which gives one person the power to end another person's additional relationships, or to disallow some specific activity. A veto may be absolute, in which one partner may reject another partner's additional relationships unconditionally, or may be conditional and used more as a way to indicate a serious problem in a relationship. Used particularly in relationship configurations where an established couple is seeking additional partners.

VINCILAGNIA: Sexual arousal from tying up or otherwise physically restraining a partner.

VIOLET WAND: One of the most common and safest of electrical play devices, the violet wand works by creating a strong static electrical field on the electrode. The violet wand feels nothing like what you might expect. Used in sensation play.

VIPER: A type of striking whip with 3 to 4 flat lashes made of thin rubber that taper to a point at the striking end.

VOYEUR: One who is excited or aroused by watching others in a sexual context.

WARTENBERG WHEEL: A metal, slightly spiked wheel typically used by neurologists to test nerve function in the skin but incorporated into BDSM play. Used in sensation play.

WANNABE: An insulting term which indicates disrespect or contempt on the part of the speaker for the person so named.

WATER SPORTS: A class of activities including but not limited to urination. Golden shower. Part of sensation play, degradation play.

WAX PLAY: The practice of dripping hot wax onto a person. The temperature of various types of waxes can vary greatly. Paraffin wax, soy wax. Common house candles should be avoided. Try to avoid scented candles or rubbing oil on the body prior to wax play. Talcum powder can be used prior to waxing to ease the removal process. The use of a drop cloth to catch all the spilled or scraped wax also helps. *Keep a fire extinguisher nearby. NEVER SPRAY A FIRE EXTINGUISHER DIRECTLY ON A PERSON; USE COLD WATER OR SMOTHER THE FLAMES WITH A FIRE RETARDANT BLANCKET.*

WHIP: Any flexible material, but usually made of leather, attached to a handle and used to strike a person. Includes floggers, single tails, etc.

WHIPPING POST: A fixed post used to immobilize a person prior to whipping or flogging.

WOLF COLLAR: A collar featuring long spikes that project outward when worn.

YOKE: A restraint device consisting of a metal bar or wooden plank, often about three feet long, with wrist-locking cuffs on each end and a neck-locking collar in the middle.

ZENTAI SUIT: A skin-tight full-body suit, often made of Spandex or a similar breathable material, that includes a full hood, most often without openings for the eyes or mouth. Such suits are often worn as part of a sexual fetish, but have also been used in various comedy videos due to their cheap cost and distinct look.

ZIPPER: A string of clothespins tied along a length of twine when placed along the body that can then be yanked off one by one or all at once.

ZIP TIE: A plastic wire tie. Cable tie.

Chapter 6:

Commonly Used Acronyms

A quick reference guide for BDSM shorthand.

- BDSM - Bondage & discipline, dominance & submission, sadism & masochism

- 420 - A universal symbol for the use of and appreciation for marijuana

- :) - Smile

- <3 - Means "Love" (If you look at it sideways, it looks like a heart)

- AA - African-American

- ABDL - Adult Baby Diaper Lover

- ABF - Adult Breast Feeding

- ADHD - Attention deficit hyperactivity disorder

- AFAB - Assigned female at birth

- ANR - Adult Nursing Relationship

- ASL - Age, sex, location

- BBC - Big Black Cock

- BBW - Big, Beautiful Woman

- BD - Bondage & Discipline

- BDSM - Bondage & discipline, dominance & submission, sadism & masochism

- BF - Boyfriend

- BHM - Big, Handsome Man

- Bi - Bi-sexual

- BWC - Big White Cock

- CBT - Cock and ball torture

- CD - Cross Dresser

- CFNM - Clothed female, naked male

- CIS or Cisgendered person - A person who identifies with the gender they were assigned at birth. Opposite of transgender.

- CNC - Consensual non-consent

- D/s - Dominant/submissive

- DD - Domestic Discipline

- DD/bg - Daddy Dom/baby girl

- DDF - Drug and Disease Free

- DILF - Dad I'd like to fuck

- Dom - Dominant male

- Domme - Dominant female

- DP - Double penetration (vaginally and anally)

- DWM - Divorced White Male

- FF - Fist fucking also called fisting

- FLR – Female-Led Relationship

- FWB - Friend with Benefits

- GF – Girlfriend, but could also mean Gender Fluid

- GG - a genetic girl; a non-trans woman, as opposed to a TG

- GL - Good looking

- GQ - Genderqueer

- GRS - Gender reassignment surgery

- GSOH - Great sense of humor

- HMU - Hit me up

- HoH - Head of Household
- HRT/SRS - Hormone replacement therapy/Sex reassignment surgery
- HRU - How are you
- HU - Hook up
- HWP - Height and Weight Proportional / Proportionate
- I<3U - "I love you"
- IDK - I don't know
- IRL - In Real Life
- ISO - In Search Of
- LARP or LARPing – Live-action roleplaying
- LDR – Long-distance relationship
- LEO - Law enforcement officer
- LG or lg - little girl
- LMAO - Laughing my ass off
- LMK - Let me know
- LRT - Loving Relationships Training
- LS - Lifestyle
- LT - Long term
- LTR - Long-Term Relationship
- M/s - Master/slave
- MD - Mommy/Daddy
- MILF - Mother I'd like to fuck
- MMA - Mixed Martial arts Aikido-a Japanese martial art
- MUAH/MWAH - The sound of giving a kiss
- MWM - Married White Male

- NB - Non-binary
- NSA - No Strings Attached
- ONS - One-night stand
- OP or O/P - Overpowered, or it can mean "Original poster"
- POT - post orgasm torture
- PDA - Public Displays of Affection
- PM - Private Message
- PnP - Party and Play
- PNP - Party n' Play
- POV - Point of view
- PTSD - Post traumatic stress disorder
- QoS - Queen of Spades
- RACK - Risk-Aware Consensual Kink
- RL - Real life
- RP relationship - Role play relationship
- RP - Role play
- RT - Real time
- SAF - Single Asian Female
- SAHM - Stay at home mom
- SAM - Smart-ass masochist
- SBF - Single Black Female
- SBM - Single Black Male
- SD/SB - Sugar daddy/sugar baby
- SO - Significant other
- SSBBW - Super-Sized Big, Beautiful Woman
- SSBHM - Super-Size Big, Handsome Man

- SSC - Safe, Sane, and Consensual

- STD - Sexually transmitted disease

- STI - Sexually transmitted infection

- STR - Short-Term Relationship

- sub - submissive any gender, any sexual orientation

- SWF - Single White Female

- SWM - Single White Male

- Tbh - To be honest

- TG - Trans-Gendered

- TiH - Taken in Hand, male-led relationship

- TPE - Total Power Exchange

- TS - Trans-Sexual

- TT - Tit torture

- TTFN – "Ta ta for now," an informal good-bye

- TTYL or ttyl - Talk to you later

- TV - Transvestite

- V-Card - V stands for virgin; holding the V-Card means you're still a virgin, or a card-carrying virgin

- V-Safe - A man who has had a vasectomy

- WAM - Wet and messy

- WIITWD – "What it is that we do" - This includes all activities that the mainstream would consider "kinky"

- WWM - Widowed White Male

- Y/O or y/o – "year old," placed after a number to denote age

Chapter 7:

Club Etiquette Tips

As more and more people enter the scene, I feel it necessary to offer up some tips on club etiquette.

1) People get into their "club head space" once they enter a club. So, with this in mind, don't get offended if you attempt to engage in a conversation with someone and they blow you off. They may not have permission by their partner to engage with strangers.

2) Never interrupt an ongoing scene between two or more people. It's normal to be curious and watch, even wanting to ask questions, but simply wait until their scene is over and give them a few moments to recompose themselves before asking.

3) Never touch someone or put your hands on anyone without them signaling to you that it's OK.

4) Never just walk over to someone's toy bag or equipment and start picking things up. They're not your toys, so ask permission first.

5) Don't be disruptive during a scene between people. Laughing, giggling, pointing, making loud or rude and judgmental comments, etc.

6) A club is not some kind of free-for-all for you to do as you wish with anyone you wish to do it with. Negotiating

and getting consent comes first.

7) Some club events are sex positive and some events are not.
The club events I have attended that are sex positive have a closed-off area for couples only. Check in with the event organizer if you have questions.

8) Most, if not all, clubs forbid photos being taken. Even if those playing were to consent to photography, those in the background of your photos may not have given you their consent to be in your photos.

9) Don't take out your cell phone and start going through it, checking for messages or for any other reason. Most clubs have an area set aside especially for this reason to prevent photography or other recording in the rest of the club. Club organizers and dungeon monitors don't know what you're doing on that phone.

10) Club events will normally have a DM, Dungeon Monitor, and/or security personnel for your safety and protection from unwanted attention. Should you experience any consent violations, report your experience to either a DM or the event organizer — and don't be shy about it either. They are there for your protection and to ensure everyone's rights are not being violated.

Notes:

_____
_____
_____
_____
_____
_____
_____
_____
_____
_____
_____
_____
_____
_____
_____
_____
_____
_____
_____

Notes:

Notes:

_____

_____

_____

_____

_____

_____

_____

_____

_____

_____

_____

_____

_____

_____

_____

_____

_____

_____

www.ingramcontent.com/pod-product-compliance
Lightning Source LLC
Chambersburg PA
CBHW022340280326
41934CB00006B/715